Mind Hacking

Unleashing Your Full Potential for Personal Growth

(How to change your mind for good and Unlock Your Mind's Limitless Potential)

Jose Jones

Published By **Cathy Nedrow**

Jose Jones

All Rights Reserved

Mind Hacking: Unleashing Your Full Potential for Personal Growth (How to change your mind for good and Unlock Your Mind's Limitless Potential)

ISBN   978-1-7776028-4-0

No part of this guidebook shall be reproduced in any form without permission in writing from the publisher except in the case of brief quotations embodied in critical articles or reviews.

Legal & Disclaimer

The information contained in this book is not designed to replace or take the place of any form of medicine or professional medical advice. The information in this book has been provided for educational & entertainment purposes only.

The information contained in this book has been compiled from sources deemed reliable, and it is accurate to the best of the Author's knowledge; however, the Author cannot guarantee its accuracy and validity and cannot be held liable for any errors or omissions. Changes are periodically made to this book. You must consult your doctor or get professional medical advice before using any of the suggested remedies, techniques, or information in this book.

Upon using the information contained in this book, you agree to hold harmless the Author from and against any damages, costs, and expenses, including any legal fees potentially resulting from the application of any of the information provided by this guide. This disclaimer applies to any damages or injury caused by the use and application, whether directly or indirectly, of any advice or information presented, whether for breach of contract, tort, negligence, personal injury, criminal intent, or under any other cause of action.

You agree to accept all risks of using the information presented inside this book. You need to consult a professional medical practitioner in order to ensure you are both able and healthy enough to participate in this program.

Table Of Contents

Chapter 1: Understanding The Human Mind 1

Chapter 2: The Power Of Mindfulness ... 19

Chapter 3: Cognitive Science In Mind Hacking 33

Chapter 4: Applied Psychology For Mind Mastery 47

Chapter 5: Practical Techniques For Mind Hacking 62

Chapter 6: Overcoming Obstacles In Mind Hacking 72

Chapter 7: The Journey Toward Emotional Resilience 83

Chapter 8: Mind Hacking For Improved Focus And Creativity 93

Chapter 9: Living Your Best Life Through Mind Hacking 107

Chapter 10: Embracing The Unforeseen 123

Chapter 11: Embracing Your Inner Strength 134

Chapter 12: Embrace Rewards For Achievement... 147

Chapter 13: Motivation From Within ... 165

Chapter 1: Understanding The Human Mind

2.1 Basic Structure and Functions of the Human Brain

The mind is an extremely good masterpiece of nature and the most complicated organ in the human frame. Understanding the essential form and features of the human thoughts is an important steppingstone to gaining knowledge of mind hacking. By knowledge the underlying form of our thoughts, we can higher admire the strategies that lead to our mind, feelings, and behaviors.

The human mind consists of about 86 billion neurons, every interconnected in a superb, difficult community. It is broadly divided into 3 primary regions: the cerebrum, the cerebellum, and the brainstem.

The cerebrum is the largest and maximum dominant part of the thoughts. It is cut up into hemispheres, the left and the proper, each similarly divided into 4 number one lobes: the frontal, parietal, temporal, and occipital lobes. The frontal lobe is related to better cognitive features like questioning, preference-making, and planning. It also controls our voluntary movement and has a feature in the law of emotions. The parietal lobe strategies sensory statistics it gets from the body consisting of spatial experience and navigation. The occipital lobe is on the complete liable for imaginative and prescient, on the equal time because the temporal lobe manages memory storage and processing, emotion, and expertise language.

Beneath the cerebrum lies the cerebellum. Although it is lots smaller, it includes more or less half of of all the neurons within the mind. The cerebellum is normally involved specially motor manage, but it additionally contributes to capabilities which includes interest and the processing of language, music, and exceptional sensory temporal stimuli.

The brainstem acts as a relay middle, connecting the cerebrum and cerebellum to the spinal twine. It performs many automatic capabilities which embody respiratory, heart rate, frame temperature, wake and sleep cycles, digestion, sneezing, coughing, swallowing, and vomiting.

Within the cerebrum and cerebellum is the limbic machine, regularly called the emotional thoughts. This system includes structures inclusive of the amygdala, associated with processing feelings, specifically worry and aggression; the hippocampus, key to the formation of recollections; and the hypothalamus, regulating physiological abilities like hunger, thirst, sleep, and temper.

Understanding the fundamental shape of the human mind and its key regions gives the critical context to recognize the complexity and class of our highbrow approaches. The human mind's shape is intricately designed to way, keep, and retrieve information, strength our emotions, coordinate our actions, and execute better cognitive abilties.

However, the brain is not absolutely an impartial organ running in isolation. It is constantly speaking with the rest of the body, influencing and being precipitated through our bodily fitness. This complex courting paperwork the idea for the thoughts-frame connection, a idea we're able to discover in addition in later sections.

As we transition to the subsequent part of our journey—information how our thoughts and feelings are processed—we deliver with us this understanding of our brain's form and characteristic. It gives a foundational know-how as a manner to permit us to delve deeper into the arena of thoughts hacking, equipping us with the equipment crucial to control and optimize our intellectual strategies.

2.2 How Our Thoughts and Emotions are Processed

Now that we recognize the mind's shape and its critical regions, allow's delve into the manner it techniques our mind and feelings. This elaborate technique is the very essence of our human experience, as thoughts and emotions are the the usage of forces in the back of our actions, behaviors, and alternatives.

A perception starts offevolved as an electrochemical sign inside the thoughts. When we apprehend some thing from our senses, it triggers neurons to hearth and create a belief sample, that could be a instance of the thing we're perceiving. The frontal lobe, the middle for higher cognitive skills, plays a crucial function in processing and decoding this data. It allows us to evaluate, determine, and decide how we reply to the stimuli we come upon.

Along with mind, our thoughts additionally techniques emotions. The limbic gadget, specially structures just like the amygdala and the hippocampus, is more frequently than now not involved on this technique. When we revel in an event, our amygdala assesses it for capability harm. If it senses danger, it proper now triggers a reaction, frequently earlier than the rational part of our brain even has a threat to react. This automatic, brief-fireplace response is the reason why we every so often discover ourselves reacting emotionally to events earlier than we've were given simply processed them cognitively.

What's captivating is the intimate courting between mind and feelings: they are intrinsically related and together influential. How we assume may have an impact on how we feel, and vice versa. If we constantly recognition on bad mind, we're probably to enjoy corresponding terrible emotions. Similarly, our emotional usa can colour our thoughts. When we're in a effective mood, we are more likely to have powerful thoughts.

Understanding the brain's characteristic in processing thoughts and feelings is a key hassle of mind hacking. By expertise how this approach works, we are capable of pick out the foundation of our mind and feelings, recognize why they get up, and make bigger strategies to manipulate and control them effectively.

Furthermore, it's far essential to recognize that not all of our thoughts and feelings are processed consciously. Much of what goes on in our minds takes place underneath the ground, in our subconscious thoughts. Our aware mind, responsible for our awareness and desire-making in the present 2d, simplest represents a small fraction of our cognitive interest. Meanwhile, our unconscious mind tirelessly strategies a wealth of records outside of our aware focus, storing memories, research, and ingrained ideals.

As we move into the following section, we're going to delve deeper into the area of the aware and subconscious thoughts. These dual components of our cognition play a pivotal function in thoughts hacking. Understanding their courting and their particular roles will empower us to harness the electricity of our minds correctly and definitely.

2.Three The Power of Subconscious and Conscious Minds

The human thoughts can be predicted as an iceberg. The tip of the iceberg it is visible above the water surface represents our aware thoughts, the a part of our cognition we're privy to. Meanwhile, the massive mass beneath the water's ground symbolizes our unconscious mind, a far large and influential aspect of our cognition that operates in big part out of doors of our conscious popularity.

Our aware mind is in which active wondering strategies rise up. It's in which we make decisions, treatment troubles, and exert willpower. The conscious mind is logical, analytical, and allows us to interact with the sector in real-time. It offers us with the capability to popularity our hobby and is the detail of our cognition that we're maximum acquainted with.

On the opposite hand, our subconscious thoughts is lots greater mysterious and a long way-carrying out. It works tirelessly in the information, storing and retrieving statistics, managing bodily functions, and housing our beliefs, reminiscences, and reminiscences. The subconscious mind techniques data from our senses even though we aren't consciously privy to it. This consistent, subconscious processing appreciably affects our conscious mind, emotions, and movements.

For example, deeply rooted ideals in our subconscious, frequently fashioned at some point of formative years, can considerably effect our thoughts and behaviors in adulthood. If we hold a unconscious belief that we're no longer right enough, this perception can seem in our aware thoughts as emotions of loss of self assurance or inadequacy, impacting our picks and movements.

Therefore, to genuinely master our thoughts and feelings, we need to delve into the depths of our unconscious mind. Understanding the unconscious mind and its affects on our aware thoughts and moves is a fundamental problem of thoughts hacking. It permits us to understand and venture subconscious beliefs that may not serve us properly, making manner for tremendous and beneficial concept patterns.

Additionally, the electricity of the unconscious thoughts is not restrained to influencing our thoughts and behaviors. The subconscious mind additionally continues a robust link with our bodily our our bodies, processing physical sensations and regulating physiological competencies. This mind-frame connection bureaucracy the concept of psychosomatic fitness, in which our highbrow u . S . Can impact our bodily nicely-being, and vice versa.

As we transition into the following segment, we're able to discover this mind-frame connection in extra element. Understanding this bidirectional hyperlink is crucial for thoughts hacking, because it now not satisfactory impacts our emotional nation however additionally our bodily fitness. The energy of our unconscious thoughts extends some distance beyond the cognitive realm, imparting a robust bridge among the highbrow and bodily additives of our being.

2.Four The Mind-Body Connection: A Bidirectional Link

The mind-body connection is a important concept in psychology and neuroscience that acknowledges the effective, bidirectional hyperlink among our highbrow and physical states. This concept shows that our mind, feelings, beliefs, and attitudes can undoubtedly or negatively have an effect on our natural functioning. Simultaneously, what takes location in our bodies—our bodily fitness and organic reputation—can effect our mental state.

A easy instance of this connection is strain. When we understand a chance, whether or not real or imagined, our thoughts reacts via triggering a strain response in our our our bodies, additionally referred to as the "combat or flight" response. This response prepares our our our bodies for instant movement, fundamental to physiological adjustments like extended coronary heart fee, rapid respiration, and heightened alertness. Chronic stress can motive a number of physical fitness troubles, alongside aspect coronary coronary heart sickness, digestive problems, sleep disturbances, and weakened immune characteristic. Thus, the intellectual enjoy of pressure might also have profound, tangible effects on our bodily fitness.

Conversely, our our bodies also can have an effect on our minds. Poor bodily fitness can reason an advanced hazard of developing highbrow health issues. For example, human beings with continual illnesses are more likely to enjoy depression. Similarly, practices that beautify physical fitness, like normal exercising and a balanced healthy dietweight-reduction plan, are appeared to boost mood and decrease tension and depression.

In trendy years, clinical research have begun to expose the mechanisms in the again of this connection. This studies suggests that our brains are in ordinary conversation with the relaxation of our our our bodies. For instance, the intestine, often known as the "2d mind," has a right away line of conversation to the thoughts thru the vagus nerve. This "gut-thoughts axis" has massive implications for intellectual fitness, with studies suggesting a hyperlink amongst intestine fitness and mood problems.

The thoughts-frame connection means that searching after our bodily fitness can beautify our highbrow well-being, and coping with our mental fitness can motive superior physical fitness. Mind hacking takes whole benefit of this bidirectional link. By reading techniques to control stress, along aspect mindfulness and meditation, we are capable of enhance every our intellectual and physical fitness. Furthermore, via adopting healthy life-style conduct, we're capable of bolster our intellectual resilience.

As we flow into to the following phase, we can take into account how this difficult connection impacts our behaviors and selection-making process. Understanding the strategies our mind interacts with and informs our body, and vice versa, can empower us to make healthier picks that align with our average nicely-being. This bidirectional hyperlink extends the scope of thoughts hacking past just our minds, taking off avenues to normal nicely-being.

2.Five The Role of Our Mind in Our Behaviors and Decision-making Process

The human thoughts is a very effective stress that directs our behaviors and drives our choice-making strategies. Understanding the feature that our thoughts plays inside the ones factors is crucial in successfully studying mind hacking strategies.

Our conscious and subconscious minds art work collaboratively in shaping our movements and choices. The aware mind is answerable for logical reasoning and the picks we make with interest. These selections frequently incorporate problem-solving, weighing options, and interest of capability results. On the opposite hand, the subconscious thoughts influences our behaviors based totally totally on our beyond research, ingrained ideals, and deep-seated emotions. These unconscious impacts frequently result in computerized behaviors and impulsive alternatives, occurring without our aware attention.

For example, in case you've ever determined yourself undertaking for a chocolate bar while you are careworn or disappointed, it is your subconscious thoughts at paintings, associating comfort food with emotional consolation. These computerized responses may be high fine or horrible, relying on the conditioning of our unconscious mind.

Cognitive biases additionally play a first-rate feature in our desire-making method. These are highbrow shortcuts that our brains use to rush up preference-making, however they're capable of regularly reason irrational results. For instance, the confirmation bias motives us to choose facts that confirms our pre-modern beliefs, main to selections based totally on partial facts.

Emotions are a few different key player in our choice-making system. They can every assist and save you us. On one hand, they offer precious information approximately our internal kingdom and may manual us in the direction of selections that align with our values and health. On the alternative hand, severe emotions can occasionally cloud our judgement, important to rash or impulsive choices.

Understanding how our mind shapes our behaviors and picks is a vital step inside the direction of thoughts hacking. The capability to find out while our moves are being driven through unconscious affects, cognitive biases, or emotional states allows us to intervene and align our behaviors with our aware goals.

Moreover, know-how the location of our thoughts in our behaviors and selections emphasizes the importance of nurturing our intellectual fitness. A healthy thoughts effects in wholesome alternatives. By taking steps to ensure our intellectual fitness, we also are in a roundabout way influencing our bodily health, our relationships, and normal brilliant of existence.

In the approaching chapters, we're able to delve deeper into how we're capable of actively form our thoughts, impact our subconscious mind, manage our emotions, and overcome cognitive biases. This deeper information will empower us to take control of our minds, enhance our decision-making, and in the long run stay a more desirable lifestyles.

And with that, we finish the second one financial disaster of this journey. So a long way, we have explored the foundation of our intellectual techniques, understanding how the mind works, how thoughts and emotions interact, the profound have an impact on of the subconscious, and the bidirectional hyperlink between our minds and our our bodies. This gadgets the extent for the subsequent segment, in which we begin actively making use of those principles to reshape our intellectual styles and rewrite our life's narrative. Let's deliver this facts earlier and delve into the sensible thing of mind hacking.

Chapter 2: The Power Of Mindfulness

three.1 Defining Mindfulness: What it is and What it Isn't

In a global more and more full of distractions, the paintings of being gift "mindfulness" has become a transformative exercising for loads human beings. It offers a way to reclaim our interest, quiet the noise, and completely engage with the arena round us. But what precisely is mindfulness, and equally crucial, what is it no longer?

Mindfulness, at its center, is a form of meditation rooted in Buddhist life-style that has been secularized and tailored for modern-day use. It entails bringing our hobby to the present 2d with an thoughts-set of openness, curiosity, and popularity. It's approximately becoming aware about our mind, feelings, sensations, and the environment round us without judgment or instant response.

When we workout mindfulness, we aren't searching for to smooth our minds of all thoughts—that's a commonplace false impression. Instead, we learn how to check our mind and emotions as they may be, without labeling them as 'proper' or 'terrible,' or getting stuck up in them. It's approximately noticing what's taking place within the right right right here and now, whether or not or no longer it's miles the feeling of your breath, the feel of a breeze in the path of your skin, or the mind passing through your mind.

Another misconception approximately mindfulness is that it consists of being calm all of the time. While mindfulness can truly sell a experience of internal peace, it's far now not approximately suppressing our emotions or emotions. Rather, it's far approximately acknowledging our emotions, whether they may be calm, stressful, thrilled, or irritated, and accepting them as a part of our present day revel in.

Mindfulness moreover isn't about passivity or disengagement from the vicinity. Some people mistakenly accept as true with that mindfulness encourages a shape of detachment that could bring about state of no interest inside the face of lifestyles's disturbing conditions or social injustices. On the opposite, mindfulness fosters a deeper reference to ourselves and our surroundings, permitting us to reply to conditions greater thoughtfully and efficiently. It promotes engagement and motion that is responsive, in preference to reactive.

In essence, mindfulness is a pathway to self-cognizance. It's about noticing our very private kinds of idea, how we react to stressors, how we relate to others, and how we've interaction with the arena. It brings approximately a certain spaciousness, permitting us to apprehend that we aren't our thoughts or feelings, they arrive and move, like clouds in the sky. This reputation is a crucial step in the adventure in the direction of thoughts hacking, because it paperwork the basis for studying to shape and direct our thoughts in strategies that serve our health and boom.

Understanding what mindfulness is, and what it isn't, is the first step in harnessing its electricity. As we delve deeper into the technology in the returned of mindfulness and its blessings in the next segment, you'll benefit a greater know-how of ways this historical exercise can be a realistic and treasured device within the current context, particularly in getting to know our thoughts.

3.2 The Science Behind Mindfulness and Its Benefits

In the previous few decades, technological understanding has started to entice up with historical focus, presenting compelling evidence for the transformative energy of mindfulness. While mindfulness is rooted in centuries-vintage practices, modern neuroscience and psychology have furnished a systematic basis that enables supply an cause of why and the manner mindfulness works.

Neuroscience research suggests that mindfulness workout can bodily reshape our brains. This concept, called neuroplasticity, refers back to the thoughts's capability to trade and adapt in reaction to experience. Mindfulness has been decided to reinforce neural connections in areas related to attention and emotional law, and to lessen interest within the amygdala, the thoughts's 'fear center'. This can cause higher interest, improved emotional resilience, and a discounted stress response.

Further, mindfulness has been proven to sell metacognition: the capability to do not forget one's very very own thinking. This advanced self-consciousness is the important thing to recognizing and breaking loose from everyday perception patterns and cognitive biases that could restrict our perspective and avoid effective preference-making.

Clinical psychology research has also showed a large number of mental fitness advantages of mindfulness. Mindfulness-Based Cognitive Therapy (MBCT), which incorporates mindfulness practices, has been identified as a strong intervention for preventing relapse in essential despair and decreasing symptoms in some of intellectual fitness situations along side anxiety problems, PTSD, and dependancy.

Beyond highbrow fitness, mindfulness can also confer physical fitness blessings. Research shows that ordinary mindfulness exercise can decorate immune function, reduce blood pressure, enhance sleep, and alleviate chronic ache. The thoughts-frame connection underscores those findings, suggesting that improving our highbrow properly-being via mindfulness can also need to have tangible effects on our physical health.

Additionally, mindfulness has been placed to sell empathy and compassion, enhancing interpersonal relationships. It can growth activity pride and performance, suggesting that the advantages of mindfulness bypass beyond private health to impact every sphere of our lives.

Understanding the technology within the once more of mindfulness and its myriad benefits underscores its relevance and applicability in cutting-edge existence. It gives a strong reason for incorporating mindfulness exercising into our each day workout routines, no longer actually as a pressure-bargain tool, however as a way of improving our ordinary wellbeing and ability to navigate lifestyles successfully.

In the following section, we are capable of introduce a few number one techniques to exercise mindfulness. These strategies will offer practical equipment that will help you revel in firsthand the transformative electricity of mindfulness, allowing you to begin the system of gaining manipulate over your thoughts and shaping your lifestyles in extra intentional and nice techniques.

three.3 Basic Techniques to Practice Mindfulness

Having discovered out what mindfulness is and the era at the back of its blessings, it's time to discover some easy strategies for practicing mindfulness. Mindfulness would possibly likely appear precis or tough before the whole thing, but it's far surely handy to every person and may be practiced in lots of techniques.

Mindful Breathing: This is one of the simplest and maximum not unusual mindfulness practices. It consists of focusing your interest to your breath, observing each inhalation and exhalation without in search of to control it. Notice the sensation of the air flowing internal and from your nostrils, the upward thrust and fall of your chest or stomach. When your thoughts wanders, as it necessarily will, lightly deliver your awareness again to your breath.

Body Scan: This workout includes directing your attention to precise additives of your frame, from your ft to the crown of your head. As you mentally test your frame, have a take a look at any sensations, anxiety, or ache which you stumble upon with out judgement.

This permits promote a more cognizance of your body and its connection in your intellectual nation.

Mindful Eating: Turn mealtimes proper into a mindfulness exercising through savoring each bite. Notice the feel, taste, and aroma of the food, the technique of chewing, and the feeling of swallowing. Mindful consuming can remodel an regular hobby into a exercise of being present and appreciating easy pleasures.

Mindful Walking: When on foot, supply your hobby to the sensation of your ft touching the ground, the rhythm of your steps, the motion of your body. Notice the wind in opposition on your pores and pores and pores and skin, the sounds round you. This exercise may be mainly grounding and may be completed everywhere, from a quiet wooded region direction to a bustling town sidewalk.

Loving-Kindness Meditation: Also known as Metta meditation, this practice involves silently repeating terms of goodwill for yourself and others ("May I be satisfied. May I be wholesome. May I be stable.") This fosters a enjoy of compassion and interconnectedness, enriching the first-rate of your relationships and your private properly-being.

These practices provide an area to start for integrating mindfulness into your ordinary life. Remember, mindfulness is not about conducting a nice state, however about being open, curious, and accepting of some thing arises in the gift second.

In the subsequent section, we are able to delve into how those mindfulness techniques will can help you advantage extra manage over your thoughts, a key step inside the machine of 'thoughts hacking.' Understanding the way to manipulate your thoughts through mindfulness will empower you to form your highbrow landscape in techniques that guide your chosen properly-being and the achievement of your existence goals.

3.Four How Mindfulness Can Help in Gaining Control Over Thoughts

With an statistics of clean mindfulness techniques, we are able to now find out how mindfulness right away contributes to gaining manipulate over mind, a pivotal detail in the way of thoughts hacking.

At its center, mindfulness is ready cultivating recognition. By growing a non-judgmental focus of our thoughts and feelings as they rise up, we're higher capable of understand them and their influences. This popularity is step one in concept manage, as it permits us to perceive and interrupt the automated questioning styles that frequently dominate our minds.

Automatic mind are short, regular thoughts that rise up with out aware interest. They regularly relate to ingrained beliefs or attitudes approximately ourselves, others, and the sector, and can be every immoderate high-quality and terrible. While a number of the ones automatic thoughts can be beneficial, others can purpose emotional distress or unhelpful behavior. For example, you'll possibly have an automated belief like "I constantly mess topics up," which could reason feelings of anxiety or disappointment and probable purpose avoidance behaviors.

Mindfulness allows us slow down and study those automated thoughts. By paying cautious hobby to our mind without getting stuck up in them, we are able to start to be conscious patterns. Over time, we are able to see which thoughts serve us nicely and which bring about distress or unhelpful actions. This consciousness gives us the capability to pick how we reply to our thoughts, in vicinity of reacting or habitually.

Furthermore, mindfulness fosters an mind-set of popularity and non-judgment. Often, we're able to get caught up in looking to suppress or manipulate effective mind, in particular if they may be lousy or uncomfortable. However, this conflict can surely make those mind greater persistent. Mindfulness teaches us to permit all mind and feelings to be gift without pushing them away or getting swept up in them. This creates place for extra thoughtful, planned responses.

Practicing mindfulness moreover lets in us amplify a kinder, extra compassionate relationship with our minds. Instead of harshly judging ourselves for exceptional mind or emotions, we're capable of reply with records and self-compassion. This shift in angle can be profoundly freeing, allowing us to navigate our intellectual landscape with extra ease and resilience.

Mindfulness, in essence, permits us to end up the "observers" of our thoughts instead of getting entangled in them. This does not advise we will never have poor or unhelpful mind. Rather, it method we benefit the capacity to apprehend them as quick highbrow activities that don't must outline us or dictate our actions. In the subsequent segment, we are able to observe sensible techniques to weave mindfulness practices into the material of normal existence, in addition assisting us benefit manage over our thoughts and shape our fact more deliberately.

Chapter 3: Cognitive Science In Mind Hacking

4.1 Introduction to Cognitive Science and Its Relevance to Mind Hacking

Cognitive era is an interdisciplinary subject of have a examine that explores the individual of the human thoughts and its techniques. This region converges views from psychology, neuroscience, computer technological know-how, anthropology, linguistics, and philosophy to solve the complexity of human cognition. Cognition refers back to the highbrow techniques that consist of perception, memory, understanding, language, hassle-solving, and desire-making. The records of those methods is crucial to the workout of thoughts hacking.

In its most effective shape, mind hacking is the manner of leveraging cognitive technological statistics thoughts to understand, manipulate, and enhance our intellectual abilities. Akin to a laptop hacker who attempts to gain unauthorized get right of get entry to to to a device, mind hacking consists of breaking into our cognitive patterns and reprogramming them for better intellectual health and normal performance.

As we dive into cognitive technological information, we are taking a journey into the problematic layers of our highbrow procedures. These strategies, which arise largely ignored, shape our mind, emotions, behaviors, and ultimately, our realities. By turning into privy to them, we are better organized to understand why we expect and behave the way we do. This understanding is a crucial step in gaining control of our minds.

Cognitive technological know-how enables us see our minds as complex however decipherable structures. The requirements of cognitive generation provide the conceptual system to decode the underlying mechanics of our intellectual tactics. And once we decode the ones procedures, we will manage them in methods that serve our properly-being and life dreams.

For instance, if we recognize the mechanisms of memory formation and preserve in mind, we're capable of enlarge techniques to decorate memory frequent overall performance. If we apprehend how our thoughts techniques emotions, we're capable of domesticate extra wholesome emotional responses. The same not unusual feel applies to our language, perception, choice-making, and trouble-fixing abilities.

In essence, cognitive technological knowledge lays the inspiration for mind hacking. It empowers us with the theoretical information and practical machine to take manage of our mind, remodel our intellectual styles, and decorate our lifestyles reviews.

As we delve in addition into the subsequent sections of this chapter, we are going to explore the location of cognition in our intellectual and emotional health, the impact of cognitive biases and distortions, strategies to beautify cognitive flexibility, and the way cognitive era contributes to self-attention. As we adventure collectively, we're capable of be a part of the dots amongst cognitive technological knowledge and thoughts hacking, forging a smooth route within the course of highbrow mastery.

four.2 The Role of Cognition in Our Mental and Emotional Health

In the arena of our minds, cognition reigns superb. As the seat of our expertise and the method with the aid of which we recognize and interpret the sector, cognition is a crucial determinant of our mental and emotional health. This tricky way, which includes intellectual features collectively with belief, reminiscence, and judgment, paperwork the basis of our mind, ideals, and movements. By exploring the function of cognition, we also are investigating the blueprint of our intellectual and emotional nicely-being.

At its center, cognition acts as a bridge connecting our inner mental international with the outside physical international. We get preserve of a enormous quantity of statistics from our environment every second. It is through our cognitive techniques that we clean out, interpret, and make experience of this records. If our cognition is skewed or biased, our information of the arena and our location internal it is able to additionally be distorted, main to emotional and intellectual disturbing situations.

Cognition additionally performs a key role in emotional law. Emotions are not genuinely instinctive reactions but are frequently normal with the aid of the usage of our mind and ideals. Cognitive techniques, in particular our thoughts, supply which means that that to our emotions. For instance, the identical occasion say, a chum not responding to a message can evoke precise emotions in one-of-a-type humans depending on their cognitive interpretation of the state of affairs. While one person may interpret it as rejection and feel unhappy, another might possibly honestly expect the buddy is busy and revel in unperturbed.

Moreover, cognition is crucial for powerful hassle-solving and choice-making, skills important to our highbrow well-being. The way we assume and system facts influences how we approach troubles and make alternatives. For example, an man or woman with healthful cognitive techniques can study a trouble from various views, consider severa solutions, compare the experts and cons of every, and pick out out the super course of motion. On the opposite hand, cognitive distortions, at the side of black-and-white wondering or overgeneralizing, can inhibit effective trouble-solving and reason pressure, anxiety, or melancholy.

Cognition also interacts with our self-belief and worldview. It shapes our self-idea and ideals approximately others and the sector at large. For instance, superb cognitions approximately oneself can beautify vanity and resilience, contributing to better intellectual fitness. Conversely, lousy self-cognitions can bring about low arrogance, hopelessness, and an improved chance of intellectual fitness troubles.

Understanding the ones cognitive techniques, consequently, is critical to thoughts hacking. When we hack our minds, we try to apprehend and alter unhelpful cognitive styles to enhance our highbrow and emotional health. The next sections will delve deeper into records cognitive biases and distortions, techniques to enhance cognitive flexibility, and the function cognitive technological understanding plays in fostering self-popularity every an essential piece of the cognitive puzzle that allows us to understand our minds.

4.Three Understanding Cognitive Biases and Distortions

The human mind is an incredible computing machine, however it's far not without its flaws. One of its most not unusual shortcomings is its tendency to fall prey to cognitive biases and distortions. These are systematic errors in thinking which have an impact on the choices and judgments that humans make. Understanding the ones distortions and biases is critical for effective thoughts hacking, as they often act as limitations to clean thinking and may significantly impact our highbrow and emotional fitness.

Cognitive biases are intellectual shortcuts or 'heuristics' that our brains use to make choice-making quicker and less hard. While they can be beneficial in wonderful conditions where fast picks are desired, they frequently result in irrational mind or choices due to the fact they skip rational and logical thinking. For example, the confirmation bias is a common cognitive bias in which we pay extra interest to statistics that confirms our pre-present ideals and neglect about approximately statistics that worrying situations them. This bias can limit our know-how of the area and lead us to make poor alternatives due to the fact we are not considering all available facts.

Cognitive distortions, however, are irrational, inflated thoughts or ideals that we agree with to be actual. These distortions frequently beef up negative questioning or emotions. They are usually visible in human beings with highbrow health troubles, specifically depressive and anxiety issues, but also can upward push up in ordinary life. For example, 'catastrophizing' is a standard cognitive distortion where we generally assume the worst feasible final results. This can result in vain fear, tension, and stress.

Other not unusual cognitive distortions consist of 'overgeneralization', wherein one terrible occasion is seen as a in no way-ending pattern of defeat, 'leaping to conclusions', wherein we make bad interpretations without actual evidence, and 'emotional reasoning', wherein we assume that because of the fact we revel in a sure manner, it have to be right. These distortions can drastically have an impact on our emotional u . S . A . And conduct, most important to a vicious cycle of awful mind and emotions.

Recognizing the ones biases and distortions in our wondering is the first step in the direction of cognitive restructuring, a key method in cognitive-behavioral remedy (CBT) that includes identifying and difficult irrational or maladaptive mind. However, figuring out those biases and distortions is not enough. To without a doubt grasp our minds, we need to also attempt to reduce their impact on our questioning. This requires cognitive flexibility, the capability to conform our cognitive processing techniques to stand new and unexpected conditions in our environment.

In the following phase, we will find out severa strategies to decorate cognitive flexibility. By enhancing our cognitive flexibility, we are able to efficiently counter cognitive biases and distortions, fundamental to extra rational wondering, progressed choice-making, and better intellectual and emotional fitness. We'll moreover discover how those techniques can contribute to greater self-recognition, a essential issue of a hit thoughts hacking.

four.Four Strategies to Improve Cognitive Flexibility

Enhancing cognitive flexibility, the highbrow functionality to update amongst thinking about one-of-a-kind thoughts or to recall multiple principles simultaneously, is essential for managing cognitive biases and distortions. By fostering cognitive flexibility, you're constructing a stronger, extra resilient mind able to higher choice-making and hassle-fixing. Below are key techniques to domesticate this crucial cognitive ability.

Firstly, exposure to numerous critiques and views is foundational. By stepping out of your comfort vicinity, you are compelling your mind to modify to excellent situations and viewpoints, stimulating adaptability. This need to contain travelling to new places, analyzing a cutting-edge-day language, or surely wearing out a verbal exchange with a person whose perspectives vary from yours. These research challenge the thoughts's everyday processing pathways, encouraging cognitive flexibility.

Secondly, non-stop gaining knowledge of and intellectual stimulation are important. This may also need to imply analyzing broadly, pursuing a new interest, or undertaking publications in sudden topics. By regularly tough the thoughts in this way, you're not handiest obtaining new information however moreover promoting cognitive flexibility. It's the mental equal of move-schooling in athletics.

Mindfulness meditation is some other effective tool. By focusing your hobby and getting rid of the circulate of jumbled mind crowding your thoughts, you may decorate intellectual flexibility. Mindfulness encourages you to answer in preference to react to situations, permitting greater thoughtful and various responses.

Physical exercise has moreover been shown to assist cognitive flexibility. Engaging in normal physical hobby will growth blood float to the mind and promotes the increase of latest brain cells, enhancing cognitive functioning and versatility.

Finally, proper sleep and nutrients can not be omitted. Both significantly impact brain fitness and feature. Quality sleep lets in the thoughts to rest and reset, helping cognitive flexibility, while balanced vitamins fuels the thoughts, imparting the essential nutrients for highest pleasant cognitive feature.

Enhancing cognitive flexibility is a dynamic method, requiring non-forestall workout and commitment. However, the payoff in phrases of progressed questioning, choice-making, and problem-solving capabilities may be massive, assisting in private improvement and the mastery of thoughts hacking.

In the subsequent segment, we're able to delve into how cognitive technological understanding, the understanding of our highbrow techniques in conjunction with the position of cognitive flexibility, contributes to self-reputation, a critical element in gaining manage over our thoughts and ultimately, our lives. By information the function and mechanisms of our mind, we empower ourselves to make informed selections and adopt behaviors that foster highbrow health and nicely being. This information is the cornerstone of mind hacking, as it allows us to grow to be proactive architects of our minds.

Chapter 4: Applied Psychology For Mind Mastery

5.1 The Role of Applied Psychology in Mind Hacking

When we communicate about 'Mind Hacking,' we're essentially discussing the power to govern and manual our mind and behaviors. At the coronary heart of this capability is Applied Psychology, a region that gives valuable tool for know-how and manipulating our intellectual processes.

Applied Psychology can be visible because the practical software program of theoretical mental necessities to resolve real-global troubles. It acts because the bridge among precept and exercising, imparting scientifically grounded strategies to persuade human conduct and perception techniques efficiently. In the context of mind hacking, it serves due to the fact the toolbox filled with techniques which could assist us reshape our cognition and in the long run, our existence testimonies.

A essential premise of Applied Psychology is that our behavior and thoughts aren't random or chaotic. They are lengthy-hooked up via some of affects, which include our beliefs, attitudes, emotions, and environments. By information those impacts, we're capable of begin to recognize why we suppose and act the manner we do, giving us precious insights into our very very own cognitive patterns and behavioral inclinations.

This popularity is the primary critical step towards accomplishing manage over our minds. With a heightened awareness of our mental strategies, we are capable of pinpoint areas of weak factor, come to be aware about dangerous behavior, and chart a route inside the route of favored adjustments.

Applied psychology permits us to deconstruct our thoughts and behaviors to their essential factors. Once we try this, we are able to see how every element interrelates and affects our common highbrow wellbeing. For instance, expertise how pressure impacts our preference-making or how self-perception affects our motivation stages may be an eye fixed consistent-commencing revel in. This popularity offers us with a higher draw close of our intellectual states and furnishes us with the tools to adjust our mind-set strategically.

Moreover, applied psychology equips us with masses of interventions – from cognitive-behavioral strategies to mindfulness-based completely techniques – that may be at once implemented to 'hack' our minds. These techniques can help us overwrite destructive cognitive scripts, reshape our idea styles, and cultivate a more immoderate best, resilient mind-set.

In essence, Applied Psychology provides us with a roadmap to our non-public minds. It demystifies the reputedly complicated techniques of belief and conduct, imparting realistic strategies to regulate them successfully. By information and the use of mental concepts, we will decorate our ability to navigate the tough terrains of the mind, paving the way for a fulfillment mind hacking.

As we improvement into the following sections of this bankruptcy, we'll delve deeper into precise intellectual theories that underpin conduct exchange, discover the dynamics of motivation, power of will, and addiction formation, and unveil terrific techniques to govern and transform our mind. Along the adventure, we're going to additionally communicate real-lifestyles case research demonstrating a achievement mind hacking using accomplished psychology, solidifying our information of this transformative scenario.

5.2 Psychological Theories Behind Behavior Change

In our quest to recognise our minds, it is paramount to understand the highbrow underpinnings of behavior exchange. After all, mind hacking is ready remodeling our questioning and conduct to better serve our goals. To understand this, we will find out some pivotal mental theories that shed mild on how and why behavior exchange takes location.

Social cognitive Theory:

The first precept to take into account is Albert Bandura's Social Cognitive Theory (SCT), which highlights the interactive nature of private elements, environment, and behavior. According to SCT, our conduct is encouraged by the usage of way of our environment and private evaluations, and vice versa. A exceptional element of SCT is the idea of self-efficacy – our notion in our capability to gain a selected state of affairs. When we receive as true with we are able to alternate, we are more likely to reap our favored goals, underscoring self-efficacy as a crucial issue in mind hacking.

Transtheoretical Model:

Another essential model is the Transtheoretical Model (TTM) of conduct alternate, advanced with the useful resource of Prochaska and DiClemente. The TTM suggests that people development through a chain of six degrees while enforcing a state-of-the-art conduct or discarding an vintage one precontemplation, contemplation, guidance, action, protection, and termination. Recognizing which diploma we're in lets in us to tailor our thoughts hacking strategies for optimum effectiveness.

The Cognitive Behavioral Therapy:

The Cognitive Behavioral Therapy (CBT) model takes a barely terrific approach. It posits that our thoughts, feelings, and behaviors are interconnected. By changing our idea styles (cognition), we are capable of adjust our feelings and moves. CBT includes recognizing and hard unhelpful mind and reframing them into greater adaptive ones. This makes CBT a valuable device for mind hacking.

Further, operant conditioning, as proposed thru B.F. Skinner, illustrates how behaviors are determined out and changed through the years through rewards and punishments.

Positive reinforcements (rewards) encourage conduct repetition, at the same time as punishments discourage it. This precept shows that providing ourselves with rewards for desired behaviors and results for undesired ones can assist in using conduct alternate.

Self-Determination Theory:

Finally, the Self-Determination Theory (SDT) with the resource of Deci and Ryan affords belief into motivation behind behavior exchange. It emphasizes the position of intrinsic motivation, the force that comes from indoors, and extrinsic motivation, that is derived from outside rewards or outcomes. According to SDT, fostering intrinsic motivation consequences in more sustainable and significant conduct exchange.

Understanding the ones theories permits us to recognize the complex manner of conduct change and understand that our route to thoughts mastery isn't linear, however a dynamic, evolving journey. Armed with this understanding, we are able to method mind hacking with a greater nuanced, flexible perspective.

In the upcoming sections, we are able to dive deeper into the intricacies of motivation, energy of thoughts, and addiction formation, and discover the intellectual techniques that can help us harness those forces for effective mind hacking. Through this lens, we are able to leverage psychology now not only to understand ourselves higher but also to consciously guide our behavior inside the route we choice.

5.Three Understanding Motivation, Willpower, and Habit Formation

While the preceding segment shed mild on the highbrow theories in the back of behavior change, the focus now turns to a few key pillars of mind hacking: motivation, strength of mind, and addiction formation. These factors are the the usage of forces that assist us provoke, hold, and embed the modifications we desire in our lives.

Let's begin with motivation. Derived from the Latin phrase 'movere', meaning 'to transport', motivation is the pressure that initiates, guides, and continues goal-orientated behaviors. The types of motivation, intrinsic and extrinsic, which we've stated within the context of Self-Determination Theory, play a important function in our behavior. Intrinsic motivation springs from the pride or satisfaction derived from the hobby itself. Extrinsic motivation, as an alternative, arises from the selection to gain a reward or avoid a punishment. When aligned, the ones kinds of motivation may be powerful catalysts for trade.

Next, we've were given were given power of mind, often described because of the truth the functionality to delay gratification, resisting brief-term temptives to satisfy prolonged-time period dreams. Willpower is type of a muscle; it is able to be reinforced with everyday workout, but it can moreover end up fatigued at the same time as overused. It's a finite useful useful resource that want to be strategically managed. Numerous studies, inclusive of those regarding the famous "marshmallow test", highlight the importance of strength of will in accomplishing desires. It's the pressure that propels us in advance while motivation wanes.

The zero.33 pillar, addiction formation, is the system by using the use of way of which new behaviors emerge as automated. If you instinctively reach for a toothbrush as quickly as you awaken, you've got were given a properly-established habit. While motivation and strength of mind can kick-start our journey inside the path of exchange, conduct help hold this transformation ultimately. As the saying goes, "motivation receives you commenced out, dependancy keeps you going." The technique of dependancy formation consists of a 'addiction loop', as proposed via Charles Duhigg in his ebook 'The Power of Habit', which incorporates a cue, a everyday, and a reward. Understanding and manipulating this loop is essential for growing and converting behavior.

These 3 components motivation, self-control, and addiction formation paintings together in our quest for behavior exchange. Motivation ignites the spark, electricity of thoughts keeps the flame alive, and conduct make sure it turns into a normal, comforting fireplace. While motivation allows us start the race, power of thoughts and behavior assist us forestall it.

Understanding the interaction of motivation, power of will, and habit formation can empower us to strategically plan our adventure within the course of thoughts mastery. In the approaching sections, we are capable of delve into the intellectual strategies that might help us manage our motivation, enhance our strength of mind, and strategically shape new behavior. These techniques will assist us not quality manipulate but moreover change our thoughts, thereby main us in the direction of a success thoughts hacking.

five.Four Techniques from Psychology to Control and Change Thoughts

Building upon our information of motivation, strength of will, and dependancy formation, allow's find out a few practical techniques from psychology that would help us benefit control over our mind and allow alternate. These strategies, sponsored with the resource of rigorous studies, offer effective methods to apply what we have located about mind hacking up to now.

Cognitive Behavioral Therapy (CBT): CBT is a nicely-hooked up highbrow approach that entails identifying terrible or harmful idea patterns and actively going for walks to update them with extra healthy ones. It operates underneath the perception that our mind, feelings, and behaviors are intricately connected, and through converting one, we're capable of impact the others. For example, with the aid of reframing a self-defeating concept like "I generally fail" to "I did now not succeed this time, but I can attempt another time", we're capable of surely effect our emotions and actions.

Mindfulness-Based Cognitive Therapy (MBCT): An extension of CBT, MBCT combines traditional cognitive treatment strategies with mindfulness practices. It encourages us to turn out to be aware about our thoughts without judgment, to test them as brief intellectual sports in vicinity of real representations of reality. This heightened popularity can assist save you the spiral of terrible wondering regularly related to strain, anxiety, and melancholy.

Self-Talk: Our internal speak or self-communicate considerably affects our feelings and behaviors. Positive self-communicate, which entails encouraging and maintaining ourselves, can decorate our temper, increase our self guarantee, and increase our resilience. Techniques like affirmations and visualization, wherein we mentally rehearse awesome conditions or outcomes, can assist in this regard.

Biofeedback: Biofeedback strategies involve learning to govern physiological approaches which include coronary coronary coronary heart rate, muscle anxiety, and thoughts waves to enhance mental and emotional fitness. These techniques, frequently used on the facet of mindfulness, can enhance our ability to regulate our thoughts and emotions.

Exposure Therapy: Often used for overcoming fears or phobias, exposure therapy entails step by step and time and again exposing oneself to a worry-inducing item, situation, or idea in a controlled, stable surroundings. Over time, this may reduce the worry response and help humans benefit mastery over their thoughts and reactions.

Each of these techniques offers a completely precise technique to thoughts hacking, and their effectiveness can range counting on character factors consisting of man or woman, non-public statistics, and the nature of the mind one wants to govern or change. It's often beneficial to check with a couple of techniques or use them in conjunction to discover what works great for you.

As we development in the direction of the final segment of this bankruptcy, we will have a take a look at case research that illustrate how the ones techniques were effectively implemented in actual-life situations. These recollections of transformation and growth characteristic effective testomony to the functionality of achieved psychology in mind hacking. The journey in the direction of mind mastery is a difficult but worthwhile one, and expertise the ones strategies can be an vital step in that journey.

Chapter 5: Practical Techniques For Mind Hacking

6.1 Guided Meditation and Visualization Techniques

Our journey into sensible thoughts hacking strategies starts offevolved with guided meditation and visualization strategies. These practices stem from ancient recognition, tracing their roots returned thousands of years to Eastern philosophies. Today, present day generation affirms their performance in reworking our minds and, with the useful resource of extension, our lives.

Guided meditation is a exercise in which an character is verbally guided via a narrator or instructor right right into a state of rest. The narrative is regularly laced with soothing and non violent imagery, designed to occupy the mind and loose it from distraction, strain, and tension. The right now effect of this thoughts-frame rest is palpable, however it is the prolonged-term consequences that underscore its significance in mind hacking.

Regularly engaging in guided meditation has proven promising outcomes in improving recognition, decreasing tension, and fostering a favored enjoy of well-being.

Visualization strategies goes hand-in-hand with guided meditation. Visualization consists of growing colourful highbrow images, regularly of an aspirational nature. For instance, you may visualize your self assignment a specific purpose or embodying a tremendous man or woman trait. The mind might now not differentiate lots amongst actual and imagined scenarios; as a result, the manner of visualization efficiently trains the brain closer to a favored state or conduct. It's a effective tool for non-public development and has been used correctly with the resource of athletes, entrepreneurs, and artists alike.

Both guided meditation and visualization techniques make the maximum the plasticity of our mind, its ability to alternate and adapt with revel in. In essence, those practices mould the mind's neural pathways, effectively rewiring it to facilitate the increase we desire. This reshaping manner is slow, requiring consistency and patience, but the outcomes are remarkably transformative.

When we meditate and visualize, we faucet into the subconscious layers of our mind, the same layers that dictate a whole lot of our automatic behavior and emotional responses. By integrating the ones practices into our each day wearing sports, we essentially gain the gear to rewrite a number of the scripts in our subconscious mind, changing them with narratives that serve us higher.

As we transition into discussing cognitive reframing within the subsequent section, we will see that those practices aren't remoted strategies however as an opportunity important components of a holistic mind hacking toolkit. They contribute to the wider gadget of reshaping our cognitive structure and converting our mind, in the end changing our lifestyles. This interconnection amongst particular strategies is one of the maximum vital ideas to undergo in thoughts as we hold to discover the sector of realistic mind hacking.

6.2 Cognitive Reframing: Changing your mind, changing your lifestyles

Cognitive reframing is a effective highbrow method that consists of converting the way we interpret and recognize occasions, due to this immediately influencing our reactions and feelings. It's a middle element of cognitive-behavioral remedy, an powerful treatment for a big sort of intellectual fitness troubles, but its capability benefits enlarge a long way past the medical realm. Cognitive reframing is a great tool in the thoughts hacking toolkit, allowing us to proactively shape our mental research and elegant life first-class.

The fundamental principle inside the returned of cognitive reframing is that our mind shape our reality. This is a center situation we have got got reiterated inside the direction of this ebook, and proper right right here, we see it in motion. We're now not passive observers in the theater of our minds; we are energetic people, able to trade the plot at will. Cognitive reframing permits us to do precisely that thru hard our mind and ideals, encouraging us to see subjects from wonderful angles, and selling extra wholesome cognitive styles.

This approach includes figuring out horrible or unhelpful thoughts, called cognitive distortions, and actively going for walks to view them in a greater sensible or beneficial way. The reframing manner can be as easy as spotting that a hard scenario is short or seeing a setback as an possibility for growth. But it's miles no longer approximately developing a fake experience of positivity; it's approximately forming a greater balanced and powerful mind-set.

Regularly running in the direction of cognitive reframing can purpose profound adjustments in our emotional health, resilience, and essential life satisfaction. It strengthens our cognitive flexibility, a critical talent we're capable of discover in extra depth later. But clearly as guided meditation and visualization help reshape our neural pathways, cognitive reframing requires constant exercising to be effective.

Although cognitive reframing may be self-guided, the involvement of a professional therapist can be rather beneficial, especially in the early stages. A expert allow you to become aware of cognitive distortions you couldn't be aware of and guide you through the reframing gadget. As you broaden extra snug with the method, you could start making use of it independently, little by little constructing a greater empowering concept sample.

As we retain to discover neurofeedback and mind education sporting sports, hold in mind how the ones practical strategies interlink. Cognitive reframing and brain schooling goes together, every goal at refining our thoughts and reshaping our brains to facilitate healthier intellectual patterns. The beauty of mind hacking is on this interconnectedness, each method strengthening and complementing the others, forming a whole method to analyzing our minds.

6.Three Neurofeedback and Brain Training Exercises

As we hold our adventure into mind hacking, we attain an exciting intersection of psychology and era: neurofeedback and mind training bodily video games. These superior techniques provide new dimensions of records and manipulate over our minds, complementing and amplifying the effect of practices like guided meditation, visualization, and cognitive reframing.

Neurofeedback is a shape of biofeedback that makes use of real-time shows of brain interest, most usually via electroencephalography (EEG), to train self-law of mind features. In other terms, it lets in us to look and regulate the workings of our brain as they arise. When we will see our brainwaves, we can attempt to control them, training our brains to carry out in more desirable and inexperienced techniques.

In a median neurofeedback consultation, sensors are positioned to your scalp to degree electrical interest. You then engage with a computer program that responds on your brainwaves. For instance, the program can also moreover praise you with factors or development in a exercise while your brain operates in favored frequencies, subtly encouraging your mind to copy those styles.

Brain schooling wearing sports activities, rather, do no longer require specialized generation. They are cognitive duties designed to beautify precise mind features, like reminiscence, hobby, processing velocity, and hassle-solving capabilities. These wearing occasions often take the shape of video games or puzzles and can be executed using a smooth pen and paper or through committed apps and online structures.

Research has proven that every neurofeedback and mind schooling bodily sports can yield tangible advantages. Neurofeedback has been used correctly to deal with conditions like ADHD, anxiety, and sleep issues. It also can beautify focus, reduce stress, and boom commonplace cognitive function. Similarly, thoughts education sports activities sports had been proven to decorate numerous cognitive talents, and a few research propose they may even dispose of the onset of dementia symptoms.

As we transition to discussing Neuro-Linguistic Programming (NLP) strategies for thoughts manipulate, hold in mind how these strategies interplay. Each thoughts hacking method we are exploring, which encompass neurofeedback, mind training wearing activities, and NLP, gives precise equipment to manipulate our cognitive techniques. Together, they form a wealthy toolbox for mind mastery, permitting us to tailor our thoughts hacking journey to our personal dreams and needs.

As we further our know-how of the mind and its workings, the significance of this sort of diverse method will become more obvious. Whether we are actively reframing our thoughts, visualizing our best selves, training our brains, or utilizing NLP, we are making strides toward more effective, planned manage over our minds. The shared give up-aim is undertaking greater highbrow fitness, cognitive regular performance, and an enriched statistics of us.

Chapter 6: Overcoming Obstacles In Mind Hacking

7.1 Common hurdles in the adventure of mind hacking

As you embark at the transformative journey of mind hacking, it is critical to count on the hurdles you can encounter alongside the manner. Understanding the ones disturbing conditions can prepare you for the endurance and patience required to build mastery over your very own thoughts.

One of the first hurdles is skepticism. The human mind is inherently conservative and has a tendency to face as much as new mind or practices that don't in shape inside its cutting-edge understanding. Some may additionally moreover moreover locate the concept of 'hacking' one's own thoughts unbelievable or intimidating, proscribing their willingness to completely have interaction with the strategies and techniques stated in this ebook. Overcoming skepticism calls for an open thoughts and a hobby approximately the potential of 1's non-public mental capabilities.

Secondly, expectations can also function a stumbling block. Many people assume instantaneous effects after they begin making use of latest strategies, and the absence of on the spot transformation can bring about discouragement. As we stated already, Mind hacking isn't always an overnight approach; it requires ordinary workout, time, and attempt. Understanding and accepting that development can be slow and non-linear can assist overcome this hurdle.

Another commonplace obstacle is loss of self-reputation. To efficaciously hack our minds, we want to first recognize our mind, feelings, and behaviors — and this can be uncomfortable. It requires us to confront additives of ourselves that we may opt to forget approximately. Furthermore, figuring out our cognitive biases, concept distortions, and unhelpful styles of thinking can be hard, mainly with out steering.

Next is the project of inconsistency. Just as physical muscle groups want regular exercising to become more potent, the thoughts desires consistent exercise to exchange. The busy nature of modern lifestyles can make it hard to find time for those practices. Some people might also moreover start enthusiastically however then permit their practices slide while existence gets busy or annoying. Consistency is fundamental in thoughts hacking, and finding a manner to include those techniques into your each day normal may be a large project.

Lastly, the hurdle of dealing with bad feelings can be especially daunting. Mind hacking includes searching at and jogging with our thoughts, with a view to usually convey us face-to-face with terrible emotions. Learning to sit down with those emotions, in preference to fending off or suppressing them, is a crucial a part of the approach, but it could be hard and ugly.

These are a number of the not unusual hurdles in the adventure of mind hacking. However, whilst the ones obstacles may additionally seem bold, recollect that they may be part of the manner. Overcoming them isn't only feasible but can purpose extra self-information, resilience, and highbrow mastery. In the following phase, we're able to delve into particular techniques to cope with resistance and setbacks on this journey.

7.2 Techniques to cope with resistance and setbacks

Just as a physical journey encounters tough terrain and setbacks, so does the adventure of mind hacking. Here, we will introduce techniques to navigate those bumps in the street.

Mental Flexibility: One of the number one steps to overcoming resistance is to broaden intellectual flexibility. This refers to our capability to shift our thoughts and adapt our behaviors in response to changing situations. Cognitive flexibility may be superior thru constantly hard our thinking styles and being open to new perspectives.

Self-Compassion: When setbacks arise, it is simple to be tough on oneself. However, self-criticism can be counterproductive, feeding proper into a cycle of negativity. Self-compassion consists of treating oneself with kindness, spotting that mistakes and setbacks are a part of the human experience. Practicing self-compassion can assist soften resistance, lessen tension, and encourage us to hold transferring beforehand.

Mindfulness: Mindfulness can help us to turn out to be privy to and be given resistance with out turning into beaten through it. It lets in us to observe our mind and feelings non-judgmentally, promoting a extra balanced reaction to demanding situations. Regular mindfulness meditation can help cultivate this skill.

Persistence: When confronted with boundaries, staying power is top. Remember that exchange isn't often linear and it's far everyday to experience americaand downs. Having an prolonged-time period mind-set can help hold motivation via difficult times.

Seek Support: You do not need to navigate this journey by myself. Enlisting the assist of a highbrow fitness professional, a mentor, or a supportive network can offer guidance, encouragement, and responsibility.

Reframing Techniques: Cognitive reframing is a effective device to cope with setbacks. This involves figuring out and tough terrible or unhelpful mind and converting them with more powerful, tremendous ones. Reframing can shift our perception of a setback from a 'failure' to a 'gaining knowledge of opportunity'.

Healthy Lifestyle: A balanced weight loss plan, regular exercising, and enough sleep can guide highbrow properly-being, resilience, and cognitive function. These way of life factors can decorate our potential to address resistance and setbacks.

Goal Setting: Clear, practicable desires can provide route and motivation. It's critical to do not forget that desires ought to be flexible, bearing in mind adjustments as wanted. Celebrating small wins alongside the way can improve motivation and make the adventure extra amusing.

Remember that those techniques are not a brief repair; they require regular software through the years. As you navigate this journey, there will unavoidably be moments of soreness. However, as we are going to explore in the subsequent segment, studying to navigate terrible emotions and thoughts is a vital detail of thoughts hacking.

7.3 Navigating Negative Emotions and Thoughts

Dealing with horrible feelings and mind is one of the maximum amazing demanding situations in the journey of mind hacking. However, navigating the ones disturbing situations is a crucial capability in shaping our minds to serve us, in administrative center in competition to us.

Recognizing Emotions: The first step in dealing with awful emotions is reputation. Emotions are like signposts, signaling some component approximately our inner u . S . A . Or our interpretation of an external state of affairs. Learn to apprehend those emotions, collectively with tension, sadness, or anger , with out judgment. Mindfulness techniques, as stated in advance, can assist with this.

Understanding the Origin: Once diagnosed, it is important to apprehend the beginning of those terrible emotions and thoughts. Often, they'll stem from beyond reviews, fake ideals, or cognitive distortions. Journaling can be a useful tool to discover and clear up these threads.

Reframing Negative Thoughts: Once diagnosed and understood, cognitive reframing can transform terrible mind. For instance, rather than thinking, "I normally fail," a reframed notion may be, "I've had setbacks, but I've additionally had successes and I can analyze from each." This shift no longer simplest adjustments our notion however can also modify our emotional responses.

Acceptance and Compassion: Sometimes, the maximum recovery reaction to awful emotions is recognition. Instead of resisting or suppressing what we sense, we will famend our feelings and reply with self-compassion. Just as we might empathize with a pal who is suffering, we are able to learn how to increase the same kindness to ourselves.

Emotional Regulation Techniques: There are severa strategies to alter emotions, together with deep respiratory, present day muscle rest, and grounding strategies. Regular exercise of these techniques may want to make them greater efficiently reachable in instances of emotional distress.

Cognitive Behavioral Techniques: Cognitive Behavioral Therapy (CBT) gives precious tools for coping with horrible feelings and thoughts. Techniques along facet perception information, behavioral experiments, and exposure hierarchies may be useful. While CBT is typically done with a therapist, a number of these techniques may be self-directed with appropriate guidance.

Professional Support: If awful emotions and mind sense overwhelming, trying to find assist from a intellectual health professional is vital. Therapies like CBT, Eye Movement Desensitization and Reprocessing (EMDR), or Dialectical Behavior Therapy (DBT) may be very effective.

Incorporating the ones strategies into your mind hacking journey can help in navigating terrible emotions and thoughts. As you make more potent your resilience and decorate your cognitive flexibility, you may be higher equipped to address outside influences on the thoughts, the project we are going to explore in the next phase. As you keep the journey of thoughts hacking, take into account that development might not continually be linear, and this is first-rate. Each step, even the setbacks, is an vital part of the journey.

Chapter 7: The Journey Toward Emotional Resilience

eight.1 Understanding Emotional Resilience and Its Benefits

Emotional resilience is a effective, multifaceted bring together that holds the capability to convert our lives. It refers to our functionality to conform to disturbing conditions or crises and rebound from adversity. Far from a easy idea of 'durability,' emotional resilience encompasses the dynamic tool of utilizing highbrow and emotional sources to navigate the spectrum of existence's opinions.

Emotional resilience is an inherent part of our human revel in and a vital element of our highbrow and emotional health. However, it isn't a difficult and rapid function; it can be cultivated and stepped forward upon thru specific techniques and strategies, a concept we can delve deeper into inside the subsequent sections.

The advantages of fostering emotional resilience are significant. It promotes mental properly-being and guards in the direction of intellectual fitness problems which includes anxiety and despair. When we are emotionally resilient, we're higher ready to address strain, which in flip minimizes its negative influences on our bodily fitness.

Resilience allows us to maintain a high satisfactory outlook and live hopeful at some stage in difficult times. It lets in us to hold problems in thoughts-set and not be overwhelmed through them. In the face of adversity, resilience guides us to tap into our strengths and gain out for manual at the same time as desired, thereby fostering private boom and gaining knowledge of.

Moreover, emotional resilience has a big characteristic in our interpersonal relationships. It fosters empathy, statistics, and endurance, allowing us to better manage conflicts and hold more healthful relationships. At paintings, emotional resilience can make contributions to higher process satisfaction and higher overall performance.

In essence, emotional resilience serves as an internal compass, guiding us thru the stormy seas of life. But it's far crucial to be conscious that resilience does not advocate avoiding or suppressing feelings. It technique experiencing, acknowledging, and expressing emotions effectively even as continuing to move ahead.

Understanding the significance of emotional resilience is step one in our adventure. As we navigate further, we are capable of discover how thoughts hacking techniques may be leveraged to cultivate emotional resilience, paving the manner for a more balanced, fulfilling lifestyles.

The subsequent segment, will show the robust device and strategies to harness your inner strength, nurture emotional resilience, and bring about transformational modifications to your existence. We can be discussing how those techniques, starting from meditation to cognitive reframing, allow you to expand a more resilient mind-set. By integrating these strategies into your regular life, you may learn how to reply instead of react to lifestyles's demanding situations, thereby enhancing your emotional resilience. So, allow's maintain our adventure inside the route of a greater resilient self.

eight.2 Techniques to Build Emotional Resilience via Mind Hacking

Building emotional resilience entails handling each our cognitive strategies and emotional responses. Mind hacking gives an to be had toolkit for fostering emotional resilience, allowing us to navigate the complex landscape of our minds efficaciously.

One of the foundational strategies for building emotional resilience is mindfulness. By cultivating a non-judgmental popularity of our thoughts, emotions, and research, mindfulness lets in us to disengage from dangerous cognitive styles and emotional reactivity. It permits us live focused inside the present second, preventing us from being swept away through stressors or succumbing to tension about the destiny.

Next, the technique of cognitive reframing allows us adjust our perspective on hard situations. Instead of viewing adversities as insurmountable limitations, we learn how to see them as possibilities for growth and studying. By consciously moving our idea styles, we're capable of extensively have an effect on our emotional responses and behavior, bolstering our emotional resilience.

Another method revolves spherical self-compassion. Often, even as confronted with troubles, we can be harsh critics of ourselves, exacerbating our pressure and emotional turmoil. Mind hacking encourages us to workout self-compassion, fostering an inner talk that is type and supportive in region of judgmental. This shift allows create a stable highbrow area, fostering recuperation and resilience.

Breathwork is each one-of-a-kind effective mind-hacking method. Deep, managed respiration physical activities can elicit the frame's rest reaction, countering the physical and intellectual outcomes of pressure. It now not only calms the mind but additionally promotes emotional readability and a revel in of manage, key factors of resilience.

Finally, we want to bear in thoughts that emotional resilience may want to not suggest a solitary journey. Mind hacking also encourages trying to find assist from others. Whether it is sharing your feelings with depended on people, turning into a member of a supportive business organisation, or searching out expert assist, don't forget that accomplishing out isn't always a sign of vulnerable aspect, however a powerful resilience-building method.

As we pass in advance, we can discover how emotional intelligence ties into this communication in segment 8.Three, "Role of emotional intelligence in emotional resilience." Emotional intelligence substantially impacts our functionality for resilience, and understanding its function can provide similarly insights into improving our emotional resilience. Remember, emotional resilience isn't always a static country but a non-stop adventure. With the ones strategies in hand, you're well-organized to navigate this course, cultivating emotional resilience thru the strength of thoughts hacking.

eight.Three Role of Emotional Intelligence in Emotional Resilience

Emotional intelligence (EQ) is a essential component that underpins emotional resilience, supplying us the capabilities to navigate adversity with extra ease and effectiveness. Emotional intelligence is the capability to understand, understand, control, and use emotions in constructive and adaptive approaches. It plays an critical position in constructing emotional resilience via way of influencing how we tool emotions, react to stressors, and interact with others.

Understanding one's feelings, a key detail of emotional intelligence, permits us to widely recognized our emotions with out judgment. It allows us to view our emotional stories as valid and meaningful factors of our human enjoy, in vicinity of as weaknesses. This recognition is crucial to constructing emotional resilience. Recognizing emotions as they stand up creates an opportunity for conscious response in preference to a reflexive reaction. This shift in mind-set lets in us to answer to tough situations with more thoughtfulness and calm, fostering emotional resilience.

Managing feelings successfully is each other detail of emotional intelligence. It consists of our capability to stay composed and controlled, even in the face of adversity. When we are able to alter our emotional responses, we're higher prepared to address stressors that come our manner. Additionally, being able to modulate our emotional reactions can save you the sort of rumination or catastrophic wondering that exacerbates emotional distress and hampers resilience.

Empathy, or the capability to understand and share the feelings of others, is any other measurement of EQ that contributes to resilience. Empathic humans can forge stronger connections, increase extra strong resource structures, and own a broader perspective. These developments help burn up the depth of horrific tales and foster a feel of belonging and statistics, critical factors for resilience.

Lastly, emotional intelligence includes using emotions to facilitate thinking and problem-fixing. It approach harnessing our emotions, even the ones uncomfortable or distressing, to tell selection-making and to inspire motion. This capability allows us to confront and overcome disturbing conditions more successfully, fostering resilience.

To decorate emotional intelligence, and eventually emotional resilience, you may leverage mind-hacking techniques mentioned in advance, like mindfulness and cognitive reframing. Mindfulness aids in the notion and know-how of emotions through way of selling a non-judgmental recognition of the triumphing second. Cognitive reframing allows within the effective management of emotions by the usage of manner of allowing us to regulate our views on stressful situations.

As we discover emotional resilience further inside the next section, "Emotional resilience: The key to dealing with pressure and adversity," we will delve deeper into how EQ-fortified resilience can be a effective great pal in dealing with life's demanding situations. We'll discover how emotional resilience, with emotional intelligence at its middle, can help us navigate adversity, recover from stress, and emerge more potent. With an facts of the role of EQ in constructing emotional resilience, you are higher geared up to cultivate these crucial talents for non-public growth and well-being.

Chapter 8: Mind Hacking For Improved Focus And Creativity

nine.1 The connection among mind manipulate and superior recognition

The journey of knowledge the thoughts and its severa intricacies is replete with charming insights, and a compelling detail of this exploration is the relationship between thoughts control and more best focus. In essence, thoughts manage, a powerful final consequences of successful mind hacking, can motive a big enhancement in our capability to consciousness, bringing about profound enhancements in our non-public and expert existence.

Mind control, contrary to misconceptions, isn't approximately suppressing thoughts or curtailing feelings. Instead, it is about expertise our belief styles, feelings, and cognitive biases, and channeling them to artwork in our desire. In unique phrases, it is approximately schooling our minds to feature as our best friend, in vicinity of our adversary.

Focus, inside the most effective terms, is our capability to take note of unique duties or thoughts at any given second, at the identical time as filtering out extraneous records that doesn't contribute to our instant dreams. It is a beneficial knowledge, crucial to severa cognitive abilities like gaining knowledge of, problem-fixing, creativity, and decision-making. In an era characterized via incessant distractions, an higher popularity can suggest the distinction among reaching our desires and falling quick.

Mind manipulate and popularity proportion a symbiotic dating, wherein each influences the alternative. The greater manipulate we've got were given over our minds, the easier it turns into to keep popularity and vice versa. But how exactly does thoughts manage purpose greater great reputation? Let's delve deeper.

The first step in thoughts manipulate is awareness. As we develop an information of our notion styles and cognitive biases through mind hacking, we emerge as adept at identifying distractions and pointless mind that frequently cloud our mind. With prolonged hobby, we're able to consciously pick out to focus our hobby on the responsibilities which may be clearly meaningful and useful to us.

The subsequent step is law, in which we discover ways to control our thoughts, feelings, and reactions to distinct stimuli. This manner consists of severa techniques, together with cognitive reframing, mindfulness, and meditation, which we mentioned in preceding chapters. By training those strategies, we are able to redirect our interest once more to our cognizance element every time we get distracted.

Furthermore, mind manage permits us to harness our emotional responses efficaciously. Emotions can appreciably have an impact on our capacity to attention. For instance, pressure and anxiety can scatter our interest, even as calmness and self assurance can assist us live focused. By controlling our emotional responses, we are able to create a intellectual country conducive to sustained interest.

Lastly, thoughts manage promotes intellectual resilience. Life often gives tough conditions that would derail our hobby. However, a properly-hacked mind, armed with resilience, can rapid get better from adversities, keep composure, and maintain recognition amidst chaos.

In essence, thoughts manipulate, via the technique of mind hacking, performs a crucial function in improving our cognizance. However, it's miles essential to bear in mind that that is a functionality, and like any talents, it requires exercising and consistency. In the following section, we are capable of observe how mind hacking can also increase our creativity, some other cognitive characteristic intricately associated with focus.

9.2 Mind Hacking Techniques for Boosting Creativity

Creativity, regularly associated with artists and inventors, is an innate human trait that performs a huge role in our non-public and professional lives. It's the engine of innovation, problem-fixing, and development. However, masses of us encounter blocks in getting access to our modern ability. Fortunately, thru the exercising of mind hacking, we can faucet into this dormant reservoir of innovation and creativeness. Let's delve into some thoughts hacking strategies for enhancing creativity.

The first and most important approach is cultivating mindfulness. It involves being absolutely gift in the 2d, listening to your thoughts, feelings, and environment without judgment. By watching our thoughts with out seeking to exchange, suppress, or react to them, we often encounter unexpected innovative thoughts. This method encourages divergent wondering, a cognitive technique related to creativity, associated with the technology of novel and sundry thoughts.

The workout of meditation, especially open-tracking meditation, can also stimulate creativity. Open-tracking meditation encourages a massive popularity of your environment, thoughts, and emotions without that specialize in a selected object or concept. This shape of meditation fosters cognitive flexibility, allowing us to view issues and conditions from diverse perspectives, fostering cutting-edge answers.

Neurofeedback, a sort of biofeedback that gives actual-time suggests of mind hobby, also can beneficial aid in enhancing creativity. By schooling our brains to access the 'alpha united states,' a circumstance of comfortable alertness extremely good for daydreaming and creativity, we will create an environment conducive to modern questioning. The real-time remarks lets in us to manipulate and advantage this country at will, giving us greater get entry to to our innovative abilties.

Another important approach is cognitive reframing. It consists of changing our perception of a hassle or a state of affairs to view it from a sparkling attitude. Often, our routine kinds of questioning restrict our creativity. Cognitive reframing disturbing situations the ones ordinary perception patterns, permitting us to suppose outside the sector and provide you with progressive solutions.

Lastly, training gratitude and high fine affirmations can decorate our creative prowess. A extremely good thoughts-set expands our idea horizon, encouraging broader, extra flexible thinking. By fostering a wonderful internal environment, we are able to get right of access to a better type of progressive mind.

While these techniques provide paths to extra proper creativity, they'll be no longer magic wands so that it will right away remodel us into modern geniuses. They require practice, staying energy, and steady try. It's furthermore essential to create an external environment that helps creativity one that evokes chance-taking, values interest, and does not worry failure.

Integrating the ones thoughts hacking techniques into our normal does greater than in reality enhance creativity. They additionally enhance our interest, as mentioned within the previous section, and resource in distinctive cognitive abilities. The key's to bear in thoughts that creativity isn't a difficult and speedy trait but a abilities that may be cultivated and advanced over the years.

In the following phase, we are going to discover how those strategies have been achieved in actual-existence situations, illustrating their realistic software in improving attention and creativity. These case studies will provide a clearer records of the transformative ability of thoughts hacking and inspire you to embark to your thoughts hacking adventure.

9.Three Case Studies: Improved Focus and Creativity Through Mind Hacking

In the preceding phase, we delved into the numerous mind hacking techniques to decorate creativity and awareness. Now, permit's explore some case studies that focus how human beings and agencies have efficiently implemented those techniques to faucet into their innovative functionality and improve their attention.

Case Study 1: A Writer's Revelation

Emma, a a fulfillment author, decided herself in a creativity drought, now not capable of hooked up writing with the identical zest she as soon as possessed. She grew to turn out to be to mindfulness and meditation to rejuvenate her innovative talents. She began thru using going for walks closer to mindfulness, consciously specializing in her gift 2nd – her breath, the keys on her computer, the phrases forming in her thoughts. Over time, Emma started to be aware a change. She observed herself writing with renewed electricity, unhampered thru the burden of her creator's block. Her thoughts, more in track together together with her inner thoughts, grow to be making connections it in no way did earlier than, making her writing greater colorful and appealing.

Case Study 2: An Organization's Transformation

Next is an example of a tech startup. To preserve a aggressive aspect within the unexpectedly evolving tech organisation, the startup had to foster a modern environment. They delivered a thoughts hacking software that concerned neurofeedback classes and cognitive reframing workshops. The personnel have been skilled to enter the alpha brainwave kingdom, diagnosed for promoting creativity and current-day questioning. Cognitive reframing workshops advocated them to venture their recurring thinking styles and method problems from a glowing attitude. The cease result modified into an apparent enhancement in the creativity of solutions and techniques devised with the aid of the team.

Case Study 3: A Student's Journey

Our final case take a look at revolves round Aaron, a university pupil suffering with awareness and interest problems, appreciably affecting his educational common performance. He determined to adopt the approach of mindfulness and notable affirmations. Every morning, he may additionally need to take a seat in silence, focusing on his breath and releasing any distracting thoughts. He complemented his mindfulness exercise with immoderate first-rate affirmations, frequently telling himself, "I am targeted. I am succesful." Over time, Aaron's interest advanced appreciably, reflecting virtually in his instructional outcomes.

These case studies highlight the transformative strength of thoughts hacking techniques. They show that with the useful resource of changing our internal idea procedures, we will significantly have an impact on our outside movements and abilties.

However, it is critical to word that a comfortable and managed mind plays a substantial characteristic in this method. Successful ideation, as visible in those instances, is predicated closely on a mind freed from chaos and distractions. In the following section, we are able to delve into this idea and recognize how a comfortable thoughts paves the manner for cutting-edge questioning, for that reason in addition strengthening our innovative prowess.

9.Four Role of a Calm and Controlled Mind in Successful Ideation

Successful ideation is the birthplace of innovation and creativity, and a relaxed, controlled thoughts is the fertile soil in which this will prosper. As illustrated by way of the usage of manner of the instances we tested inside the previous segment, this u . S . A . Of intellectual tranquility and control isn't always absolutely a pleasing-to-have : it's miles a critical problem in the technique of revolutionary questioning.

The human thoughts is frequently likened to an untamed horse, capricious, and effects distracted. In this nation, it is able to be tough to generate clean, modern mind as we're constantly getting sidetracked thru intrusive mind, stress, or mental fatigue. This is in which the concept of 'mind hacking' enters, introducing techniques to calm the mind and benefit manipulate over our thoughts.

A calm thoughts lets in us provide interest to one task or concept at a time, giving it our whole interest. This consciousness paves the way for deep belief and analysis, allowing us to connect the dots, apprehend styles, and assemble upon gift thoughts to create a few component precise. It aids in releasing up intellectual area, permitting creativity to flow unimpeded. Imagine your mind like a non violent sea; high-quality even as the ground is tranquil are you capable of see the treasures mendacity underneath.

On the opportunity hand, a managed thoughts is likewise vital for a achievement ideation. It guarantees we do no longer lose ourselves in a maze of random thoughts however observe a first rate idea machine. It continues our thinking at the proper tune, helping us constructively critique our thoughts, understand ability flaws, and devise powerful answers. With mind manipulate, we're able to guide our thoughts in a preferred route, harnessing the thoughts's complete ability to bring about progressive thoughts.

Chapter 9: Living Your Best Life Through Mind Hacking

10.1 Mind hacking for non-public boom and self-development

"Mind hacking for personal boom and self-development" is the opening consciousness of this final financial disaster. This is the end result of all the strategies, techniques, and theories we have have been given explored. It's about harnessing the power of our minds to end up the remarkable variations of ourselves, to live our lives as definitely and richly as feasible.

Understanding the thoughts is the first step in this transformative adventure. As we've visible inside the previous chapters, the mind is an problematic maze of mind, feelings, and perceptions that shape our fact. Each concept we've, every belief we preserve, has the power to each restrict us or propel us in advance. Through thoughts hacking, we recognize these cognitive strategies and discover ways to steer them in the direction of brilliant and powerful paths.

For private boom, mind hacking is a tool that can help us locate and cope with our restricting ideals, allowing us to break free from the chains of self-doubt and worry. By understanding how our mind works, we're capable of strategically rewire our thoughts to assist our goals and aspirations. For example, if we've got a fear of failure, mind hacking strategies can assist us reshape this worry proper into a powerful motivator. We can train our mind to view failure now not as a useless-forestall but as a stepping stone to success, a mastering opportunity.

Beyond overcoming awful idea patterns, thoughts hacking permits us to domesticate superb ones that encourage private increase. Visualization strategies, as cited in Chapter 6, can assist us construct a glittery, compelling photo of our favored destiny, thereby aligning our thoughts in the course of sporting out it. This imagined future can act as a beacon, guiding our options and actions inside the course of that direction.

Self-development is some other superb difficulty of thoughts hacking. It's about refining and sharpening our talents, attitudes, and behavior to beautify our commonplace awesome of lifestyles. Techniques together with neurofeedback and cognitive reframing can useful resource us in engaging in self-improvement. With the ones equipment, we are capable of beautify our reputation, manage strain correctly, and foster a increase thoughts-set that perspectives demanding situations as opportunities for mastering rather than threats.

Another vital component of self-development via mind hacking is the cultivation of emotional intelligence. A better EQ (emotional quotient) can assist us understand and manage our emotions better, improving our self-reputation, empathy, and interpersonal relationships. Moreover, it lets in us to broaden resilience, permitting us to get better from setbacks and navigate lifestyles's americaand downs with grace and equanimity.

In essence, mind hacking for personal boom and self-development is ready learning to take the reins of your intellectual tactics. It's approximately breaking a ways from computerized, unconscious reactions and adopting a proactive method to shaping your mind, emotions, and behaviors. It's about evolving into a more assured, resilient, and fulfilled individual who is on top of things in their existence and its route. This can substantially effect distinctive regions of our lives, along aspect our relationships and social interactions, which we are succesful to talk within the next section.

10.2 Impact of mind hacking on relationships and social interactions

As we keep our exploration into the arena of thoughts hacking, we discover it deeply impacts our relationships and social interactions, painting them with the colours of empathy, expertise, and significant connection. These, ultimately, are the hallmarks of an enriched lifestyles, one which isn't absolutely ruled thru non-public desires however also intertwined with the threads of social bonds.

Our interactions with others reflect our internal country of thoughts. If our minds are turbulent, it's likely to arise in our relationships, inflicting misconception, conflict, or distance. On the opportunity hand, a peaceful and controlled thoughts can bring about more wholesome, more nice relationships. Herein lies the overall performance of thoughts hacking – it allows us to domesticate a extraordinary inner environment that right now influences our outside interactions.

An vital a part of mind hacking that bolsters our relationships is emotional intelligence. As we've were given referred to in Chapter eight, a excessive EQ lets in better expertise of our personal emotions, allowing us to speak our emotions extra effectively. It additionally enhances our capability to apprehend others' feelings, fostering empathy. This -way information strengthens the bonds of our relationships, decreasing the opportunity of conflicts and improving mutual apprehend and admiration.

Another critical aspect of thoughts hacking that benefits our social interactions is the workout of mindfulness. By being present and completely engaged in our interactions, we showcase a diploma of apprehend and attention for others, which, in flip, strengthens our relationships. Mindfulness allows us to virtually pay attention to others, as a substitute of truly looking forward to our turn to talk, selling deeper, more meaningful conversations.

Mind hacking also allows us to control and control our reactions better. This is particularly beneficial in warfare situations. Instead of responding with anger or frustration, we are able to hire mind hacking strategies to preserve a peaceful demeanor, determine the state of affairs objectively, and respond in a way that resolves the warfare in vicinity of escalating it.

Moreover, via the practice of self-reflection and self-reputation, mind hacking encourages us to widely known and address our biases and prejudices, contributing to extra healthful and greater equitable social interactions. It makes us privy to our behavior and its effect on others, encouraging us to undertake a extra information and compassionate technique.

The outstanding have an impact on of mind hacking is not confined to our private relationships. It extends to our expert relationships as nicely. Effective thoughts manage can useful useful aid us in growing higher collaboration and communique capabilities, attributes which might be crucial for a thriving paintings environment. The capability to deal with pressure and keep recognition, factors we are able to explore inside the subsequent phase, can also purpose stepped forward artwork relationships and extended productiveness.

In quit, thoughts hacking does not just contribute to non-public growth and self-improvement; it additionally improves our relationships and social interactions. By studying our minds, we are able to create more appealing connections, fostering a experience of belonging and enhancing our regular first-rate of lifestyles. This leads us to the subsequent phase, in which we're able to delve into how thoughts hacking can assist us attain a balanced and charming artwork-existence dynamic.

10.Three Achieving art work-lifestyles balance thru mind control

As we dive further into the possibilities of thoughts hacking, it becomes apparent that this exercising isn't virtually limited to enhancing non-public boom or enhancing relationships, but it may furthermore drastically have an effect on undertaking a harmonious art work-existence stability.

Work-life stability is a term that gets thrown round quite a bit, and for precise motive. In our fast-paced, achievement-oriented society, it's far smooth to fall right right into a pattern of strolling excessively, regularly at the rate of personal and familial relationships, health, or possibly happiness. At the coronary heart of accomplishing artwork-life balance lies the artwork of thoughts manipulate. As we have were given explored throughout this e-book, controlling your thoughts isn't always approximately suppression, however as an opportunity approximately guidance and subject.

The key to conducting work-life stability is mindfulness, an essential a part of thoughts hacking. Mindfulness can be likened to a highbrow equipment shift, permitting us to be without a doubt found in some thing challenge we're mission. Whether it's far operating on a assignment or spending time with own family, mindfulness we should us actually interact with the undertaking handy. It discourages multitasking, a addiction that regularly results in pressure and burnout, and encourages us to allocate dedicated, undisturbed time for every element of our existence. This manner, we ensure that we're giving our fine to each assignment and every moment, fostering productiveness, and pride.

Another thoughts hacking approach pivotal for artwork-existence stability is pressure manipulate. Stress is inevitable, but how we deal with it determines its impact on us. Techniques together with meditation, exquisite affirmations, visualization, and cognitive restructuring can help us control stress, enhance our recognition, and maintain our intellectual fitness. By adopting those techniques, we're capable of save you art work-associated stress from spilling over into our private life, keeping the sanctity of our off-art work hours.

One crucial element in accomplishing paintings-existence balance is putting boundaries, a project that becomes much less hard with progressed self-focus – a fruit of mind hacking. As we turn out to be extra attuned to our desires and boundaries, we can set and keep barriers extra effectively, actually defining our art work time and personal time. This, in turn, helps prevent burnout and ensures that we are dedicating accurate enough time to our personal existence.

Mind hacking moreover encourages us to undertake extra healthy conduct, including ordinary exercising, a balanced food regimen, and excellent sufficient sleep. These behavior make a contribution extensively to our normal properly-being, making sure that we aren't certainly strolling efficiently however also living healthily. This holistic method to well-being is the essence of accomplishing art work-existence balance.

Lastly, mind hacking promotes a growth mind-set, helping us recognize that it is ok to now not have the entirety decided out and that each task is an opportunity for increase. This mind-set alleviates hundreds of pressure that we often positioned on ourselves, permitting us to approach work and lifestyles with a greater cushty and first rate perspective.

In conclusion, mind hacking gives numerous tools which can beneficial resource us in undertaking a right paintings-lifestyles stability. It's approximately guiding our thoughts to make alternatives that foster our nicely-being, productiveness, and contentment. As we transition into the subsequent phase, we're capable of delve into the lengthy-term blessings of mind hacking and the way it contributes to health, happiness, and achievement.

10.Four Long-term benefits of mind hacking: Health, happiness, and success

The promise of thoughts hacking isn't always a fleeting improvement or a quick increase in productivity. Rather, it's a lifelong willpower to self-improvement and self-attention, whose quit end result take vicinity in severa varieties of prolonged-time period advantages: appreciably health, happiness, and success.

Let's start with fitness. Physical fitness and highbrow fitness are intricately associated. By practising thoughts hacking strategies, we cultivate higher strain manage abilties, principal to lower blood strain, advanced digestion, and better sleep patterns. Moreover, a clearly pressured mind will instinctively make greater healthful alternatives, be it vitamins, exercising, or enough rest. Techniques like mindfulness could make us more attuned to our body's desires, permitting us to answer because it need to be and thereby promoting everyday physical fitness.

Now, onto happiness. A large part of thoughts hacking revolves spherical hard horrible idea styles and cultivating positivity. Through strategies like cognitive restructuring, meditation, and affirmation, we teach our thoughts to focus on the best, thereby fostering a greater extremely good outlook on lifestyles. This highbrow shift is crucial in cultivating happiness. Moreover, as we discover ways to live more in the gift 2d via mindfulness, we're able to derive more satisfaction from our each day research, similarly enhancing our happiness quotient.

Fulfillment is a few other prolonged-time period benefit of mind hacking. Fulfillment is an precis idea, top notch for every character. However, it basically indicates a sense of pleasure or final touch. By harnessing the electricity of our minds, we come to be more focused on our dreams and extra attuned to our passions. This attention and reputation can guide us to align our actions with our personal and expert objectives, main to a profound experience of fulfillment.

Another problem of success this is greater suitable through way of mind hacking is the fulfillment derived from relationships. As we come to be extra self-aware and emotionally clever, we moreover come to be better at handling our relationships. We turn out to be extra empathetic, know-how, and patient, leading to deeper, more meaningful connections with the human beings around us.

Lastly, mind hacking empowers us to be the wonderful versions of ourselves. It nurtures our growth thoughts-set, encourages us to step out of our comfort zones, and propels us toward continual analyzing and self-development. This everyday evolution and growth are probably the maximum enormous long-time period gain of mind hacking, contributing to a fulfilling and enriching life.

The benefits of mind hacking are manifold and profound. But they require persistence, staying power, and clearly, a dedication to the way. Mind hacking isn't a brief restore; it is a lifelong journey of self-discovery, boom, and transformation. As we discover within the final segment, committing to non-prevent thoughts hacking exercise is essential for reaping the ones lengthy-term blessings and simply living your exceptional existence.

Chapter 10: Embracing The Unforeseen
Synopsis

Chapter explores the significance of welcoming and correctly responding to sudden sports to your journey inside the path of fulfillment. It emphasizes that, regardless of cautious planning, you can't manipulate the whole lot that lifestyles throws your way. The bankruptcy advises readers now not to rush their reactions to the sudden, encouraging them to view it as an opportunity to expose them instead of as a roadblock. By adopting this attitude, humans can construct a reservoir of past victories over demanding situations, fostering extra resilience and self-self notion.

Furthermore, the financial disaster highlights the significance of no longer viewing the unexpected as a private assault, as many human beings have a propensity to do. It underscores that the sudden ought to be regarded as a chum, no longer an enemy, and a trainer in preference to a destroyer. When approached with this attitude, even completely glad, surprising activities may be harnessed to reinforce up development inside the route of one's goals, exemplifying the essence of Mind Hacking.

Now which you've grasped the importance of setting realistic but tough small desires to your journey to achievement, it is time to speak approximately a few aspect crucial: your constrained manipulate over attaining the ones desires. Yes, it's far actualyou do not have complete manage over your future. No depend how meticulously you propose, how many colourful sticky notes adorn your workspace, or how many journals you fill together along with your dreams and improvement, existence will despite the fact that throw sudden surprises. There might be twists and turns on your lifestyles's narrative, virtually as there are for all of us. How will you respond to those sudden occasions, a number of which may also check your intellectual resilience if you're wound too tight? This financial ruin will discover a way to welcome the surprising, a important issue of Mind Hacking. Here are numerous techniques to live composed and encompass the sudden trends that may first of all appear like threats however can in the long run make you a stronger, greater resilient individual:

No depend how difficult it may revel in even as you are blindsided via unexpected facts, constantly bear in thoughts that the next day is a state-of-the-art day. It's crucial to keep angle inside the route of these tough moments; time might now not stand though, even even as you get preserve of scary information like a technique loss or a breakup. Tomorrow will arrive, permitting you to resume your adventure toward success due to the fact the pain from this surprising setback lessens and also you regain hobby. As noted in advance, it's far essential no longer to take pleasure in self-pity at the same time as faced with adversity. Additionally, you have to in no manner, underneath any activities, consider that you deserve unfortunate sports, a not unusual misconception many humans adopt whilst managing tough times. Such a faux perception has no vicinity in any way in Mind Hacking.

Ask your self what you could study from this unexpected development. View the ones jarring moments as teachers. What is

the lesson to draw from the lack of life of a cherished one? What did that individual educate you? What would probable that person want you to do as you still collect a terrific existence and profession? This is a superb thoughts-set, in place of honestly dwelling in the emotional dumps and no longer seeing any mild. Your first query whilst the boss tells you that personnel cutbacks have included you want to be: What will I test from this?‖

When the sudden takes an poor flip, which it regularly does, it is important to keep in mind that a number of the most a hit human beings within the international have placed extra from their disasters than their successes. For instance, Abraham Lincoln confronted numerous electoral defeats before turning into president, and Thomas Edison encountered hundreds of failed experiments on his path to inventing the moderate bulb. This pattern extends to countless done folks who effects attest that failure turn out to be a beneficial trainer. Instead of viewing the unexpected as an insurmountable impediment, regard it as a realistic mentor. By adopting this mind-set, you can include the shortage of absolute manage over the entirety and avoid pointless fretting.

The people who have completed greatness did now not allow failure to shatter their self-picture. They virtually exquisite amongst their losses and their unshakeable perception in themselves. This separation is a crucial concept in Mind Hacking, highlighting the significance of keeping one's vanity however setbacks.

Recognize that one detail you can manage is your response amongst all the components of life you cannot manage. This is an age-vintage statistics we might not usually need to renowned, but it endures because it holds right! Nothing and no one can steal your functionality to maintain a amazing thoughts-set as you pursue greatness. Many wealthy marketers emphasize the significance of a extremely good mindset. They adamantly refuse to permit the unexpected derail their pursuit of goals. They have a attitude that echoes the concept: search for an open window when one door closes. Often, the unexpected gives itself as a closed door. Take a step decrease again, well known this reality, and then deliberately pick to exert greater effort on that door or are looking for out a window. This is exactly what a success people do in preference to lingering inside the hallway, grieving, and believing that the area is conspiring toward them or that they may be unworthy of open doorways.

Reframe the surprising as a stimulating assignment. To witness actual trade in your life and profession, you could want to summon your internal Bulldogthe energy of will no longer to surrender with out issues. This is one reason smaller desires are maximum first rate; on the identical time as you fall quick of them, it's easy to choose your self up, disregard the dirt, and strive all over again. So, at the same time as you are informed that there are not any available positions at the subsequent, better rung of your organization's ladder, do no longer renounce yourself to thinking, "I'll in no way make it there." Instead, proclaim, "This is a assignment I will conquer." As you correctly deal with undertaking after challenge, yourself-self assure will flourish, like a bodybuilder's bicep growing stronger. Anyone intending to alternate their life need to include disturbing conditions in area of include seeking out the precise manner out. Part of the essence of Mind Hacking is developing a passion for demanding situations that assist you to display your self in vicinity of assuming that existence ought to be with out problems.

When you embody the sudden as a friend in location of an enemy, you notice it as a precious possibility to prove your self and confront a brand new challenge. You assemble a reservoir of beyond victories over obstacles with each a success stumble upon. When confronted with the contemporary unexpected twist, you do now not even pull away. Instead, you declare, "I've conquered situations like this earlier than, and I'll do it yet again. Nothing will deter me from becoming a financial institution president." However, in case you turn away from worrying situations and lament the sudden with questions like "Why me? Why now?" your records will lack times in which you overcame limitations. This can pork up a horrible self-photograph and lead you to just accept as proper with you are a loser and a sufferer. It all hinges on how you technique the surprising

as a chum or foe, a instructor or a nuisance, a project or an obstacle. The desire is yours, and that is a few element you could control.

Take it slow at the same time as you locate yourself in a dance with the sudden. There's no need to offer you an answer for each trouble that arises. You might not spot the open window for your first appearance, and that is flawlessly high-quality. It may additionally additionally need to take days or even weeks to mull over the surprising. Take some time, but preserve the mindset that you can find out a way to consist of the sudden into your pursuit of goals in choice to permitting it to derail you. Avoid impulsive picks, like quitting your interest or shifting, proper now after encountering the sudden. Give your self time to digest it, contemplate the manner to approach the state of affairs, after which make a relaxed, rational choice. While you may in the end need to transport away your company if possibilities are dwindling, wait to do so unexpectedly upon hearing a quarterly shareholders document. People with strong self-perception are assured that, with enough time, they will discover a way to expose the unexpected to their benefit.

While reflecting at the unexpected, it's essential not to miss the opportunity that you could have performed a function in its incidence. You can not control each condition in the universe, and clearly each person claiming in any other case isn't being honest. However, when you have been the primary man or woman laid off in the route of a round of technique cuts, ought to there were a cause within the lower back of it? Perhaps it became due to the fact you have been continuously overdue to paintings 3 days out of 5 or resisted being a set player. This is some other manner the surprising can function a precious teacher. It can display that we have a few degree of manage over our destiny and that the "surprising" could have been foreseeable due to our movements or failure to fulfill particular requirements of behavior.

Lastly, an essential hassle of embracing the unexpected is recognizing that it's miles no longer a personal attack in competition to you. Many human beings erroneously come to this give up, and it hampers their development towards identifying their ability. When the surprising enters their lives, they may expect that a few "strain" is working in the direction of them or that the gambling gambling cards in no manner fell in their pick out. These horrific attitudes can steer you off path as you attempt to reach your small objectives and gain the fulfillment you aspire to.

Always recollect: the sudden ought to be seen as your best friend, no longer your adversary, a trainer, or a destroyer. And if the surprising brings wonderful newslike a boom, the assertion of a toddler on the manner, or a marriage conceptyou can modify your small objectives and larger targets for even swiffer achievement. This is Mind Hacking at its fine.

Chapter 11: Embracing Your Inner Strength

Synopsis

Chapter Three delves into the important detail of power of thoughts to your adventure to fulfillment. Willpower is the highbrow electricity that emerges via the principles of Mind Hacking. It's the force that empowers you to make disciplined selections and withstand temptations that might save you your development. Building strength of mind calls for sacrifices and energy of mind, however it's vital to accomplishing your goals. By announcing "no" to quick-time period gratification in choice of lengthy-term profits, you're making stronger your power of will muscle, which will become more resilient and unstoppable through the years.

This monetary wreck emphasizes the significance of physical movements to domesticate power of will, together with attending seminars, saving coins, and preserving power of will in difficult conditions. It highlights that strength of will is about greater than being wonderful but constantly making correct alternatives and resisting the traps that would derail your development. Visualizing your preferred future and the extended-time period benefits of your selections can be a incredible tool for reinforcing your willpower. Ultimately, this bankruptcy emphasizes strength of will's valuable feature to your journey to success and encourages you to encompass and nurture it as an essential element of Mind Hacking.

You may not permit life's surprises throw you off your route to success. Your electricity of thoughts is part of your ability to address unexpected demanding situations, which we'll delve into on this financial disaster. So, what is strength of will? Different humans may also have first-rate thoughts, but permit's think about it as intellectual electricity you may construct the usage of the ideas from this e-book. In special phrases, willpower is the strength that comes from operating towards

Mind Hacking effectively. How are you capable of improve and increase it? Let's find out the concept of self-discipline, and right here are a few steps you may take to completely embody it:

To extend your self-control, you could want to make some sacrifices. This approach, for example, putting away your video game to study a financial ruin on enhancing your thoughts. It way pronouncing no to those 3 tempting doughnuts at artwork to stick to your healthy dietweight-reduction plan (we will speak this within the subsequent financial ruin). It additionally method focusing on one character whilst you have got a exquisite concept of who you need to spend your existence with in desire to dating round. Sacrifices might be difficult first of all, but they help you construct strength of mind, making you stronger and more prepared to advantage your goals.

Similarly, you'll must exercising electricity of mind frequently to reinforce your electricity of thoughts. It way staying that extra hour at paintings to finish a further undertaking in order to impress your boss in preference to proper now becoming a member of your friends for Happy Hour. It manner attending a control seminar on a lovable weekend in preference to heading to the beach. These are examples of power of mind that will help you construct your strength of will. As you examine to say "No" to the splendid things to mention "Yes" to the higher subjects, you may discover it receives much less tough to face up to many temptations that used to restriction your development and gradual you down.

Another way to boost your energy of thoughts is by means of way of resisting the urge to react negatively while there can be anxiety on the administrative center, or you're tempted to offer a person a piece of your thoughts, either verbally or thru an e mail. It also can revel in fine to speak your thoughts inside the brief term, but it can seriously disrupt your adventure toward fulfillment in the long run. That 10-minute outburst or fiery electronic mail could have lasting outcomes. It is going into your report, and , you're now not seen as "control fabric." Was it nicely nicely really worth it? No. Part of strengthening your willpower includes jogging in the direction of power of mind, mainly at the same time as you're confronted with surprising disturbing situations or hard humans.

Don't allow the concern of failing keep you again. Instead, take formidable movement and recognise that even if you do fail, it can be a stepping stone to fulfillment, a valuable lesson. If you're analyzing this eBook, you could have battled self-doubt. In that conflict, you are in all likelihood afraid of together with extra failure in your heavy load. It's important to prevent viewing failure as greater luggage and start seeing it as a trainer, similar to how we noted the surprising in the previous economic spoil. Once you overcome your fear of failure, you'll gain the willpower to take decisive movements at crucial factors in your existence's journey: providing in your big specific, launching that element commercial agency, or asking for a boost and promoting. Willpower and a worry of failure cannot coexist.

To manual your power of will, it is critical to take concrete, actual-global moves. Although this eBook focuses on Mind Hacking, now not all of the steps are handiest intellectual; many contain tangible moves. However, it's miles critical not to intentionally placed yourself in tempting conditions. For instance, in case you're trying to shed pounds, visiting bakeries to check your remedy via exposing your self to charming points of interest, sounds, and smells isn't always encouraged. Instead, your location want to be tied to realistic movements. To improve your strength of will on the same time as pursuing personal growth, maintain a file of your efforts to illustrate commitment. For example, you can e-book a niche at a super questioning seminar next month, supply your huge superb flowers to boost your courting or open an IRA on the monetary institution to practice steady saving to your prolonged-term monetary properly-being. These actions require strength of mind and, over time, will help it expand, displaying that it isn't always quite a great deal wishing for more treatment however actively cultivating it through actual-worldwide steps.

Building and strengthening your self-discipline is critical within the early tiers of your adventure in the direction of non-public boom. Initially, it'd feel like an underused muscle with little energy. You want to constantly exercise your subject and willpower to increase it, like schooling a gymnasium power. Over time, your self-control will rework proper proper into a robust, unbreakable stress. Early on, as you attempt to benefit your small goals, you need to accentuate your issue to make certain success.

This manner is similar to beginning a healthy dietweight-reduction plan: in the initial days, you may crave carbohydrates, bread, or chocolates, relying on what you are abstaining from. However, as time passes, those cravings little by little decrease. Similarly, as your energy of will grows, you obviously end up more disciplined and a higher model of yourself. This strength of mind will keep to gain momentum until it turns into an unstoppable stress. Remember that everyone has moments of weakness; you can succumb to indulgences like doughnuts, anger, pettiness, or selfishness. Recognizing your mistakes, data that a string of slip-u.S.A. Of americacan veer you off route, and immediately getting back on course.

Willpower does no longer recommend being actually free of weaknesses; as a substitute, it is about continuously making smart alternatives and resisting the horrific mindsets and traps that might lead you off beam. For instance, giving in to the temptation of 3 doughnuts might in all likelihood re-ignite your yearning for sweets. You must bodily distance your self from doughnuts for numerous weeks to stay heading within the right course. This isn't absolutely to expose your power but due to the truth you've got each brief- and prolonged-term wants to gather. If you hold indulging in doughnuts, you can now not shed the ones five pounds this month, and you may now not in all likelihood discover many monetary group presidents who are seventy five pounds obese. In every the fast and long term, you need to face up to the temptation of 10 a.M. Snacks within the smash room. Just because it's to be had does no longer suggest you need to eat it. The flavor is not well properly well worth sacrificing your goals.

If you are not struggling with weight problems and studying this eBook, allow's do not forget another not unusual manner to test your self-control. Imagine this: you've got a few coins left over out of your paycheck, and you are tempted to shop for a ultra-modern pair of shoes. It's an real test! Willpower way resisting the urge to walk through the mall or down the town road with tempting shoe preserve suggests. Instead, you may deposit that $100 into your economic savings account, getting prepared to your small commercial company release in some years. Willpower regularly requires a rational purpose to thrive and doesn't paintings nicely for the ones driven absolutely via emotions. You should wholeheartedly do not forget that now not searching for those footwear will make contributions on your brief-time period (saving $ hundred/month) and long-term (launching a small organisation) dreams. In many strategies, strength of mind includes sacrificing immediately pleasure for long-lasting happiness. This idea contradicts what society often preaches, but it holds real. A 50-365 days marriage is usually a long way greater attractive than a 5-yr one destroyed through an affair, which normally leads nowhere excessive first rate.

Strengthen your strength of will with the aid of pronouncing no to a functionality romantic associate's advances, saving coins instead of splurging on new footwear, and deciding on yogurt over doughnuts. And in case you appear to slide up and face results, keep away from falling into the lure of believing that the universe is conspiring in competition to you. You need more than this terrible thoughts-set to attain your dreams. For example, if your boyfriend hasn't referred to as in 4 days due to an irritated outburst within the route of your ultimate telephone conversation, it's not the celebs aligning in the direction of you; your actions have to change. Your relationship isn't progressing as you would really like, and your dream of marrying him and beginning a circle of relatives is at hazard. It's no longer approximately celestial forces; it is approximately you and your choices. When you discover it tough to keep willpower, recall trying this approach:

Devote a few moments to imagining what your great life will appear like a decade from now. Picture your region, sports, and relationships. You might also additionally moreover see your self in a spacious suburban house with a loving husband and youngsters, efficaciously coping with your thriving domestic-based totally industrial corporation. In the destiny, you may experience a harmonious balance among art work and family life even as having the economic way to have amusing with each moment. Realize that attaining that dream company includes saving $two hundred monthly for the next 5 years. When you're tempted to splurge on the ones footwear that would eat up half of of your supposed monetary financial savings for the month, envision that cute suburban home together together with your circle of relatives accumulated around the fireside. Buying the boots won't bring you toward that vision; it's going to simplest keep away from your improvement. Visualizing your favored destiny can be a effective tool for bolstering your electricity of thoughts. When you regularly envision in that you need to be, it's going to can help you make the right options for your day by day existence. We'll delve deeper into this exercise of visualization in Chapter Five. Embrace and nurture your strength of will; a important factor of Mind

Hacking propels you alongside your adventure.

Chapter 12: Embrace Rewards For Achievement

Synopsis

This bankruptcy delves into the significance of profitable yourself for reaching your huge and small goals. As you navigate the direction of self-improvement and personal boom, you may stumble upon moments at the equal time as the area spherical you may now not offer the popularity or reward you deserve. This monetary damage emphasizes the significance of acknowledging your non-public achievements and celebrating your development. Doing so boosts your motivation and maintains a pleasant outlook in your adventure within the course of achievement. The bankruptcy also highlights the critical connection amongst bodily fitness and highbrow well-being. Maintaining a balanced weight loss program, exercise often, and staying hydrated are vital to sell physical and mental well-being, increase productiveness, and enhance energy stages.

As you absorb those thoughts of Mind Hacking, you will find out that treating yourself with small rewards is a manner of putting forward your development and sustaining your pressure. The financial ruin encourages you to embody a way of life that values vicinity and entertainment, showing that pursuing success need now not be a joyless assignment. By profitable your self on your achievements, you can grow to be more able to overcoming barriers, keeping motivation, and experiencing satisfaction as you figure in the direction of your favored lifestyles goals. This concept emphasizes the significance of acknowledging and celebrating your successes.

You've been diligently setting and reaching your small desires, reinforced thru your developing self-control and newfound self-belief. Those vintage lousy voices that used to name you "stupid" and "lazy" are fading away. You're witnessing your self-self guarantee and arrogance upward push each day, and you're starting to in reality accept as real with for your functionality to gain your last purpose: the life you've estimated for yourself. Now, permit's communicate about a extra thrilling hassle of Mind Hacking: rewarding your achievements.

While there can be no guarantee that those spherical you could broadly recognized your development and efforts, it is important to understand that outdoor reputation is best on occasion drawing near. Your amazing different, buddies or perhaps your boss also can superb every now and then word your tough paintings and accomplishments. You also can skip the extra mile in the workplace without receiving the acknowledgment you deserve. In a worldwide of unsure out of doors validation, rewarding your self will become even greater essential. This would no longer suggest splurging on extravagant journeys or shopping sprees but treating yourself to a small reward even as it's miles properly-deserved. This exercise is a crucial deliver of extremely good motivation, assisting you live resilient notwithstanding barriers as you pursue your dreams.

When we reflect onconsideration on worthwhile ourselves, it frequently includes indulging in a pleasant meal or making a selected buy. While those treats have their location, averting the misconception that this eBook encourages common all-you-can-eat buffets is critical. Instead, permit's commit some pages to discussing the crucial characteristic of physical fitness to your journey to fulfillment.

Here are properly-hooked up medical facts that intertwine with Mind Hacking: First, your mind is not separate out of your frame, as you may see in a sci-fi film. It's intrinsically associated on your physical nicely-being. These information are: a) Maintaining a healthy healthy dietweight-reduction plan and getting normal sleep is critical for working at your bodily top notch, which, in turn, permits you to be at your intellectual pinnacle; b) Consistent exercise acts as a supply of electricity, providing you with the power wanted as you try to build up your dreams. Let's dissect the ones critical physical requirements as critical components of Mind Hacking.

Your mental electricity is in reality critical, however even the mightiest minds can falter while plagued thru not unusual contamination, malnourishment, fatigue, or disorientation. A mentally robust man or woman suffering with bodily issues might not effortlessly wield their energy of mind, nor will they warmly consist of the unexpected whilst tired. You've likely skilled firsthand how the bodily dimension can notably impact the mental and vice versa. This may not suggest that sheer self-control can remedy illnesses, but it underscores that physical well-being profoundly influences intellectual acuity.

Consider the skyrocketing income of electricity beverages worldwide in contemporary years; greater people are attempting to find a highbrow gain, resorting to strength liquids or even sure pills as shortcuts to sharpen their minds. However, the ones measures are non-obligatory. By well caring to your frame, you may harness your intellectual faculties to their whole ability, eliminating the want for synthetic aids.

On the flip issue, an inadequate food plan and a sedentary way of life can bring about a chronic america of exhaustion, compromising your immune device and rendering you more prone to contamination. This, in flip, interprets to accelerated periods of difficult paintings absence. The perpetual feeling of being run down also can cause despair, a much cry from the course you envision to reach your dreams. Indeed, your frame and thoughts are intricately interconnected. Even in case you diligently exercise the thoughts noted in this eBook, you need to be aware of your physical health to keep away from despondency and avoid you from accomplishing your desired lifestyles.

So, how need to you approach weight-reduction plan, sleep, and workout? Amid the clamor of infinite diets vying for hobby, the important standards of retaining bodily nicely-being have remained everyday over time.

By the way, even though you may break out with a tough-driving, immoderate-partying way of life for some time—staying out till four and displaying up at the workplace at 8—it eventually catches up with you. It is probably potential on your 20s; a few can control it of their 30s, but retaining the sort of way of life in your 40s and beyond is nearly not viable. So, if you're thinking about prolonged-time period dreams and the Big Prize, it's miles clever to undertake correct health habits early to avoid drastic changes as your metabolism slows down and your joints creak. Now, permit's delve into the facts of the proper food regimen essential for maintaining your mental sharpness and not unusual fitness.

As part of Mind Hacking, permit's method the trouble of healthy dietweight-reduction plan with a awesome mindset. Instead of seeing it as a restrictive, burdensome project, recollect it as fueling a immoderate-overall performance vehicle—your frame. Just as you would not positioned the wrong sort of gas right into a sports sports car, you have to attention on offering your body with nourishing, top notch energy. We're not proper here to berate you for occasional slip-ups; as an possibility, we encourage you to continuously enhance and exercise the willpower you've got been developing. A single meal off track is not the cease of the arena, in particular if you preserve a wholesome diet. With that during thoughts, proper right here are some suggestions that will help you keep a nutritious food plan, enhance your physical health, and raise your energy levels for top performance:

Stay hydrated thru eating water regularly. While it could no longer sound exciting, it's miles critical to your fitness. Opt for water over caffeinated liquids or energy beverages, as those can dehydrate you. Aim to drink more than one glasses of water each day, prioritizing it over soda, coffee, or tea. If you crave some taste, you could find out severa calorie-loose flavored waters in stores to preserve subjects exciting.

Don't pass breakfast—it's miles more exciting and useful than it can sound. Eating inside the morning can considerably decorate the way you experience at some point of the day. Studies advise that this meal units the tone to your day, enhancing alertness, kick-starting your metabolism, and preventing unstable snacking. Without breakfast, you would in all likelihood attain for merchandising tool snacks or leftover cake, which could negatively effect your strength levels. So, what need to you eat? Doctors advise complete-grain cereals and bread, cease give up result, and lean proteins. For a wholesome breakfast, attempt difficult-boiled eggs with whole wheat pita, oatmeal topped with fruit, or whole-grain toast with peanut butter. Sit down and characteristic a laugh along with your breakfast; the ones on-the-pass cereal bars are regularly loaded with more energy and sugars. Investing an extra 15 minutes in a wholesome morning meal ought to make a main difference to your power tiers, growing your opportunities of engaging in your small goals.

Don't overlook the significance of protein—it's far a critical detail of boosting your energy. Without sufficient protein, you can short experience fatigued. Remember those photos of malnourished children you lately determined? Their bellies might be complete of rice or a few different staple, but the lack of protein (no meat to be had) leaves them listless. You truely don't need to feel like that each day. Your body requires protein for fuel, as well as for repairing and constructing muscle tissue.

Moreover, protein takes longer for the frame to interrupt down than carbohydrates, supplying an extended-lasting electricity growth. Ensure your eating regimen consists of pretty a few protein belongings, which includes fish, bird, lean red meat, nuts, milk, yogurt, eggs, tofu, and cheese. Interestingly, a cutting-edge take a look at located that many people who efficaciously out of place weight integrated nuts and yogurt as number one additives in their weight loss plan plans.

Steer clean of the fatty carbs. While carbohydrates are critical, some diets suggest reducing them out absolutely. However, you could devour them appropriately with the beneficial aid of choosing entire grains in cereals and bread, choosing brown rice, and heading off sugary options. Opt for carbohydrate property wealthy in fiber to hold everyday digestion. You don't must take away them completely if you make clever picks in this category.

Snack to save you strength crashes. Depending on your metabolism, you may require snacks among meals, mainly if you have a rushed breakfast or skip over lunch (now not advocated). You can hold a healthful energy degree through using way of choosing suitable snacks and stopping energy slumps. The pinnacle options, as endorsed with the aid of the use of way of dieticians, encompass yogurt with fruit, combined nuts, veggies with hummus, cheese, and protein shakes. While a number of the ones can be greater convenient than others, they all provide additives to help stabilize your blood sugar degrees.

Incorporate Omega-three fatty acids into your healthy eating plan. This isn't always just a passing fashion; sturdy clinical proof supports the blessings of Omega-3 acids, inclusive of lowering contamination, improving temper, and stopping depression. You can obtain this tremendous acid from salmon, walnuts, tuna, and leafy veggies. Whenever possible, choose organic resources of Omega-3 in desire to dietary supplements.

Ensure you get an excellent enough amount of magnesium on your weight loss plan. This mineral is crucial in converting carbohydrates into power, so it's far vital on your body's electricity production. Include magnesium-rich meals like almonds, walnuts, Brazil nuts, whole grains, and dark inexperienced greens.

Ensure you eat an adequate huge sort of calories. Crash diets can leave you feeling tired and lethargic. Opt for a nicely-balanced healthy dietweight-reduction plan that offers the crucial energy without relying on empty energy from foods with minimal power blessings. If you want to lessen your caloric intake for weight reduction, recollect doing so step by step over an prolonged period and cause to live near your encouraged calorie diploma. Avoid drastically slashing your caloric consumption, important to low energy degrees in a few unspecified time within the future of the week.

Now, permit's speak about the importance of exercising in preserving your energy ranges. As you encompass the thoughts of Mind Hacking and devour the right substances, you have likely observed a giant growth on your power. However, no matter a properly-balanced diet, it is everyday to once in a while enjoy greater fatigued than you would like. That's in which exercising is to be had in. Contrary to what you'll probably expect, workout may want to no longer drain your electricity; it virtually adds to it.

A present day have a look at has validated that workout is more powerful than stimulants in preventing fatigue. So, the following time you're tempted to nap, don't forget going for a stroll or a moderate run. This have a look at additionally determined out that exercise can remarkably have an effect on humans with persistent medical conditions like most cancers and coronary coronary heart disorder. If exercising can enhance their power levels, sincerely think about what it can do for you! Of path, it's far not unusual to lack motivation for exercising whilst you're already worn-out. Think about the way you sense even as you first get out of bed within the morning.

Just like inside the mornings whilst it's far tough to get away from bed, you regularly experience better hastily when you begin transferring. Exercise is quite comparableusually, when you enjoy least encouraged to do it, it may have the most awesome excellent impact. You'll enjoy a lot less fatigued as you often workout and hold a wholesome weight-reduction plan. Incorporating exercising into your weekly time table can be tough, especially in advanced societies in which place of work work is common. However, it's miles a profitable attempt that could contribute to an prolonged and more healthy existence.

Forget power beverages, triple lattes, or hyped-up sports activities sports liquids to beautify your energy. Instead, recollect physical interest an funding so as to repay with multiplied strength later. Moving your frame is a higher way to experience more colourful than relying on those short fixes. Recent research have bolstered what scientists have suspected for a long term:

people who have interaction in normal workout sincerely have greater electricity. These research discovered that 90% of those who covered bodily hobby into their exercises suggested experiencing plenty an awful lot much less fatigue in assessment to a sedentary manage organization. This increase in strength become even more extensive than the impact of stimulant medicinal drugs and implemented to humans with persistent fitness situations.

This eBook will best cowl some varieties of exercising as they're vicinity and desire-established. However, the overall guiding principle of challenge at least half of-hour of energetic motion each day is valuable. If you skip over a day, maintain in mind taking an extended stroll or the usage of a bicycle at the weekend to make up for it. Sitting in an place of job chair all day won't depart you feeling revitalized; you need to consist of everyday motion into your everyday to enhance your power tiers. Numerous internet web sites can offer information on integrating 1/2-hour of every day physical hobby into your lifestyles. Doing so will keep your mind at its pinnacle, providing you with a higher risk to apply Mind Hacking standards and form your future. Now, let's cross again to worthwhile your achievements as you accomplish small and massive goals.

Remember to underestimate your ability to benefit even the maximum miniature dreams in the course of the week. Deep down, you understand that challenge these minor milestones will in the end lead to extensive transformation. It begins offevolved with that initial purpose, like enrolling in an internet route to decorate your expert competencies. Train yourself to have fun these small victories each day, a exercising a number of the sector's maximum a hit marketers have prolonged embraced. They view the each day barriers they encounter as minor hurdles to be faced and gleaned from.

As you address the traumatic situations on your existence, address yourself to a connoisseur coffee or a movie day trip with a pal as a reward. Life ought to in no manner come to be so mundane at the same time as challenge goals that we forget to experience ourselves. Mind Hacking need to in no way be perceived as a lifestyles method that strips away the a laugh! You are the tremendous pick out of what small reward could possibly suit you: a lunch out, a brand new online game, dessert with buddies this weekend, a leisurely day providing a film marathon at home, or diving into half of a charming e book. Whatever brings you delight and makes you experience content material fabric, take delight in it as a reward due to the truth really as you can pleasant control your reactions to lifestyles's demanding situations, you could make certain you get rewarded through doing it.

Chapter 13: Motivation From Within

Synopsis

In the very last bankruptcy of this eBook, the highlight shines on the power of concept and how it fuels motivation. It underscores the pivotal function of intrinsic motivation, the hearth internal that propels humans towards their goals, no matter out of doors validation or popularity. Whether you have got were given drawn concept from beyond adversity or a nurturing surroundings, this bankruptcy unveils the call of the sport to igniting the unquenchable fireside of self-motivation.

The monetary disaster introduces the transformative exercising of visualization, a way employed through way of way of Olympic athletes, renowned performers, and a success people all through various domain names. A smooth imaginative and prescient of your future cultivates emotional attachment and strain in the direction of your aspirations. This approach lets in you to expect and embody the traumatic situations, have amusing the triumphs, and navigate the sudden twists on your route to achievement. Through the energy of notion and visualization, you can maintain your motivation burning brightly, conquer limitations, and little by little art work in the direction of attaining both small and grand dreams, ultimately constructing self-self perception and understanding your desires. Welcome to the final bankruptcy of this eBook, in which we're going to explore the most excellent device in Mind Hacking: Motivation From Within. We've included critical ideas like putting doable goals, adapting to the unexpected, constructing energy of mind, and profitable your accomplishments alongside the manner. Now, we unveil the crucial component to sustained fulfillmenttraining your thoughts to be a perpetual supply of motivation. This bankruptcy reveals that the most a success human beings in lifestyles, individuals who gain their goals and live with unwavering self-guarantee, are intrinsically caused. They do no longer depend upon outside reputation, economic incentives, or reward from others to strain them ahead; their motivation is an inner stress.

In the subsequent pages, we'll delve into the mechanics of intrinsic motivation, helping you apprehend a way to harness the superb strength of your thoughts. You'll learn how to preserve your internal hearth burning, propelling you inside the path of your goals and bolstering your conceitedness. By the prevent of this financial disaster, you'll be organized with the competencies and insights had to cultivate motivation from within, making sure which you're no longer only a bystander in your lifestyles's adventure but the captain steerage your ship towards success.

Intrinsic motivation, that unquenchable fireside, can sincerely be kindled interior you, even if you did not revel in precise challenges or adversities in some unspecified time in the future of your upbringing. While a few human beings draw motivation from early life reminiscences in which they confronted barriers, discrimination, or social dangers, it's far now not the nice course to fulfillment. This bankruptcy will manual you in discovering and nurturing your intrinsic motivation, no matter your records.

You'll study that motivation isn't actually based on beyond hardships however can be cultivated thru intellectual and behavioral techniques. It's about harnessing the strength of your mind, putting easy and significant desires, and developing a deep revel in of motive. Whether you've got faced adversity or come from a supportive records, the ideas outlined on this financial ruin will empower you to mild that internal fire and turn out to be the hold close of your destiny. So, permit's dive in and release the secrets and strategies of intrinsic motivation, placing you on a route to a more pleasant and a fulfillment life.

Visualizing your chosen results is a effective method to collect goals. Think of it as a intellectual exercise consultation for success. Many a achievement humans, which includes top athletes and musicians, use visualization to decorate their normal overall performance. In essence, you do not forget in which you need to be, who you want to emerge as, and what your final success will appearance and feel like. These intellectual snap shots remind you of your desires, preserving your motivation alive and nicely.

Visualization permits you to regularly refresh your willpower and force as you attempt for ambitious targets. Visualize your course to achievement to live targeted and stimulated. This monetary ruin will delve deeper into the paintings of visualization, imparting precious insights and practical strategies to harness this approach to your adventure to fulfillment.

Creating a smooth and incredible intellectual photograph of your preferred excellence takes time and thoughtful attention. It's a method that could take time, and you may need to set apart dedicated durations to formulate this vision. This might also need to contain a weekend getaway to a quiet vicinity wherein you may mirror and plan, or it would expand often over numerous months as your imaginative and prescient becomes greater unique and described.

To begin, you ought to ask yourself what excellence way to you for my part. Does it contain a profoundly pleasing marriage, a harmonious and satisfied own family existence, monetary protection, the notion of an prolonged-held dream region, or a career that aligns together together with your passions and skills? As you acquire this highbrow practice consultation for your future, ensuring that your vision stays grounded in truth is essential. This monetary wreck will guide you through crafting a compelling intellectual photograph of your dreams, on the way to characteristic a powerful supply of motivation in your adventure within the course of excellence.

It's important to strike a balance at the same time as developing your highbrow image of excellence. While placing sensible goals that align at the aspect of your competencies and situations is crucial, growing past what seems right away attainable is in addition vital. For example, it might no longer be sensible to visualise turning into an NBA celeb in case you're first-class five'5" tall. However, you need to despite the fact that reputation on what seems practical based to your present day scenario.

Dreaming past your immediately conditions may be a powerful motivator, inspiring you to collect better and push your limits. The secret's to balance setting doable goals with allowing yourself to dream big, believing that you could accomplish greater than your beyond activities might also moreover moreover suggest. This bankruptcy will manual you in placing that balance as you enlarge your vision of excellence.

Creating a highbrow photograph of your future is honestly step one. You must damage that imaginative and prescient into realistic steps to reveal it into truth. Think approximately the stairs needed to attain your desires, from near-term to prolonged-term. Would it contain pursuing greater training, which incorporates attending college, graduate university, law university, or clinical university? Should you become a part of a nearby network, like a church, to fulfill the form of person you need? Or you'll want to devote time every day to growth a selected capability, together with education gaming, to come to be a expert player.

This device consists of cautious making plans and putting actionable, measurable targets. You can chart a clean path toward fulfillment by breaking down your lengthy-term imaginative and prescient into smaller, feasible steps. This bankruptcy will guide you in crafting a practical roadmap to supply your goals in the direction of reality.

Mental exercise consultation is a effective device to enhance your self-control to undertaking your dreams. Visualize your self taking every step inside the course of your dream, and maintain in thoughts to count on success. Picture your self taking walks hand in hand with a loving companion, with a bit of luck receiving a diploma on level, or being surpassed the keys for your dream place of work. These intellectual rehearsals have an effect to your aware mind and might profoundly impact your subconscious, strengthening your willpower to make your goals a fact.

Consistently visualizing your course to fulfillment will assist you to build mental resilience and live prompted to conquer limitations and gain your goals. This financial ruin will delve deeper into the practice of visualization and the way it can be a effective tool for reaching your aspirations.

Visualization is sort of a thriller weapon in your mind. When you vividly recollect your favored destiny, your subconscious mind pushes you in the direction of that photograph without understanding it. This harmonious collaboration amongst your aware and subconscious minds is a powerful stress for attaining your desires. Researchers have even coined "psychology as future" to give an explanation for how visualization can make your mind take delivery of as true collectively with your imaginative and prescient has already come real.

This approach isn't always constrained to lengthy-time period desires; it can work wonders for quick-term desires, even the ones definitely mins away. For example, if you're making plans a specific date, run a intellectual film of the manner you need it to unfold. Picture the whole lot from the immediately you arrive: the arrival and fragrance of your vehicle, your attire, the phrases you may say, and the precise eating place.

This mental practice consultation motivates you to smooth your car, groom yourself, and research nearby ingesting spots. It's fascinating how the ones short "films" may be so effective. As you glide through the date, your motivation grows as you witness the night time time unfold, just like your intellectual exercise consultation. This economic break in addition explores visualization and the manner it may catalyze motivation and purpose fulfillment on your lifestyles.

The power of visualization grows stronger as you approach your dreams. It often becomes the more push you need to reap them. Imagine the usage of this strong technique to all factors of your existence: mentally rehearsing your subsequent exercise, looking in advance to your upcoming paintings project, or on the point of stress your new car off the lot to have a very good time a huge advertising. While some human beings be successful without visualization, severa research endorse that it appreciably blessings maximum those who exercise it. To harness this electricity, you could want a few quiet time and area.

An inspiring instance of visualization's impact comes from actor Jim Carrey's adventure to fulfillment in Hollywood. During his early struggles, Carrey can also spend hours sitting on a hill overlooking Los Angeles, envisioning what he preferred to achieve within the city. He set a specific intention for himself: a $10 million paycheck for a destiny film position. Carrey wrote a take a look at to himself for that amount and carried it to auditions, whether or not or now not they led to achievement or not. It's crucial to study that Carrey came from a lower-middle-magnificence historic beyond. Over time, he landed step by step more distinguished roles, sooner or later earning $10 million for a single film. He should in the end coins that self-written test, a constant supply of motivation born from his deep contemplation. Similarly, you may want to spend exceptional time taking into account your existence desires and visualizing the steps to attain them. The first step is growing that assume time, some trouble we often forget about in our generation-driven technology.

The greater you visualize your adventure to achievement. However, as you define it, the extra tangible and natural it turns into on your mind. Remember that this doesn't guarantee that existence will spread exactly just like the movie you created. But in conditions wherein you may manipulate your movements, your imaginative and prescient and truth can surely align, because it did for Jim Carrey. You can optimistically prevent your process as deliberate as soon as you've got saved enough to invest in a restaurant franchise. You can endorse to the one that you love in the right manner you've visualized, right right down to the most minor info. You can maintain that difficult-earned diploma and feature fun, despite the fact that no one on your circle of relatives has ever completed college. Without a shiny intellectual picture of your preferred final results, you could spend days, even years, making plans with out taking concrete steps in the direction of your dream. Regardless of your final motive, a easy visualization of the endpoint is a powerful catalyst for movement.

Individuals who workout this form of visualization frequently unique sentiments like, "Now I see in which I want to go. I take delivery of as authentic with it's miles possible. I want to do so the next day to move toward this cause." Clearly, visualization on my own does not physically propel us into motion, but the opportunity of taking motion increases extensively when the final effects has been vividly imagined. Another benefit of visualizing the Big Prize is that it underscores the gap we need to traverse to acquire our excursion spot, providing strong motivation. Here's each distinct realistic instance of visualization's overall performance: you visualize winning your commercial business enterprise organisation's "Salesman of the Year" award, notwithstanding the reality which you war with a stutter. As you envision accepting the award certificates from your supervisor and seeing a $1,000 bonus for your financial organization account, you start thinking about what it'll take to obtain that glad finishing. You renowned for the number one time that you require good sized speech remedy to end up a a success shop clerk. Without the visualization of receiving that top honor, you may hold stumbling via earnings suggests with a stutter, incomes a modest profits for the rest of your profession. Visualization possesses a energy that manifests every proper away and over the long time, making it ideal for conducting small desires and ultimately greedy the Big Prize.

Effective visualization is a machine that engages each emotions and the mind, adding a powerful length to motivation. Emotions may be a considerable the usage of stress with regards to psyching ourselves to tackle even the maximum tough obligations on our journey in the direction of engaging in our dreams. You'll want this emotional strain to perceive obstacles as possibilities to conquer and to decorate your unwavering energy of will. Returning to the Jim Carrey instance, he did no longer in fact living room on a California hillside and fantasize about success. He labored diligently to beautify his performing abilities, sought steerage from the ones greater professional, decided completed actors honing their craft, and attended endless auditions. His visualization of fulfillment served as a beacon, preserving his motivation in the path of the years preceding his soar beforehand. A closer check the lives of successful people exhibits that nearly none skilled "in a unmarried day achievement." They invested infinite hours, frequently referred to as the 10,000-hour rule, in advance than accumulating wealth or reaching public recognition. Visualization nurtures internal motivation, the type that burns the brightest and lasts the longest, a critical precept of Mind Hacking. So, how want to you approach visualization? Here are a few portions of advice on integrating desires and visualization:

Take a moment to put in writing your dreams in an area you may keep in mind. When you try this, it frequently sparks your creativeness right away, providing a easy picture of what you are aiming for. Write those goals honestly, adding loads of specifics to make your small steps and massive dreams smooth to tune. Remember to set ultimate dates to keep your focus sharp.

Regularly evaluation those desires. Consistently checking them will help you in refining your highbrow movie and breaking down your dreams into smaller, possible factors.

As you put together for visualisation, discover the tales of people who've completed first rate goals. Discover some inspiring costs that can encourage you, especially if you have but to attain your smaller goals and are tempted to prevent. Social media structures like Facebook may be valuable for connecting with friends running inside the path in their life aspirations.

As you acquire your mental movie, whether or not it's a scene from later in the day or a imaginative and prescient 40 years into the destiny, make certain to contain a huge quantity of physical movement in your intellectual image. For example, if you maintain in thoughts purchasing a selected item you have been craving for, visualize the whole system, from taking walks into the shop, finding the issue, intending to the cashier, and making the acquisition. Customize the physical movements for your visualization to align collectively collectively together with your unique desires and aspirations.

Enhance your intellectual film by incorporating more info which consist of sounds, smells, forms of mild, or even unique people. The maximum influential visualization practitioners frequently venture themselves to engage all their senses honestly. For example, you can initiate your visualization with diffused actions, like leaves rustling under a tree, after which transition to a brilliant depiction of a selected placing, complete with the fragrance of freshly lessen grass permeating the scene. Strive to embody all of your senses for the maximum immersive visualization enjoy, even though this can require willpower and time.

Incorporate emotions into your highbrow film. If the state of affairs calls for anger, visualize your self expressing that anger and revel in the associated emotions. On the opportunity hand, if your visualization revolves around happiness, accept as true with your self with a smile and a coronary coronary heart entire of laughter as you share the records along with your colleagues which you've been transferred to a notable and preferred department in the employer. Integrating emotions into your intellectual imagery complements the intensity and effect of your visualization.

Exclude any risky factors out of your highbrow film. In your visualization, steer smooth of negative humans, emotions, and exclusive elements till they make contributions to the very last triumph of the very last scene. Generally, the reason of this exercising isn't to hobby on terrible elements; as an possibility, it's miles supposed to be a super and empowering revel in.

Once you have created your visualization, make it a every day workout. Dedicate a few minutes each day to close your eyes and immerse your self to your mental filmwhether or no longer recognition at the wedding altar, playing wonderful time with friends, or basking on a seashore after your first million-dollar achievement. You can beautify this enjoy thru narrating your visualization, together with an thrilling tale to the intellectual pix. For example, you may say, "I'm crossing the end line in my first marathon, feeling bone tired but crushed with pride and accomplishment, a depth of emotion I've in no manner professional earlier than."

www.ingramcontent.com/pod-product-compliance
Lightning Source LLC
Chambersburg PA
CBHW071444080526
44587CB00014B/1981